A PORTRAIT OF LOVE: The Loritts Family (Clockwise from upper left)
Crawford, sisters Lavonia and Elaina, Crawford, Sr., and mother Sylvia.

"*Crawford is one of the best earthly examples of one who walks his talk. If you read this book and get nothing of significant value from it call me and I'll give you back what you spent for it!*"

DR. RALEIGH WASHINGTON,
Vice President of Reconciliation
Promise Keepers

"*Never Walk Away is a powerful and motivating story of the legacy Crawford Loritts, Jr. inherited from his father. This father-son story transcends the normal fare. It will indelibly etch itself onto your heart and remind you that fathering is best learned by example. I commend my good friend Crawford for sharing with all of us these essential truths of godly living. This is one of those rare books you won't put down.*"

JOSEPH M. STOWELL, President
Moody Bible Institute

"*Never Walk Away speaks to my heart. The mixture of timely biblical truths and personal experiences is the type of clear communication our generation yearns for. Far too often we let our precious memories fade away. Crawford Loritts reminds us that past treasures can continue to be valuable for generations to come.*"

JERALD JANUARY, SR.,
Author, Minister & Founder
The Urban Block Party

NEVER

Lessons on Integrity from

WALK

a Father who Lived It

AWAY

CRAWFORD W. LORITTS, JR.

MOODY PRESS

CHICAGO

All Scripture quotations are taken from the *New American Standard Bible,* © 1960,
1962, 1963, 1968, 1971, 1972, 1973, 1975, and 1977 The Lockman Foundation,
La Habra, Calif. Used by permission.

ISBN: 0-8024-2742-1

5 7 9 10 8 6 4

Printed in the United States of America

*This book is dedicated to my mother, Sylvia Loritts,
who for fifty-three years was the life partner and source
of strength for the greatest man I have ever known. . . .
And to my sisters, Elaina and Lavonia,
who also are "the living legacy to the leader of the band."*

CONTENTS

ACKNOWLEDGMENTS

The idea to write this book was planted in my mind more than ten years ago by a dear friend, Bobb Biehl. It took a while, Bobb, but here it is.

I am especially grateful to Steve Wamberg, who was my partner in this project. Thanks for helping me to put my thoughts, words, and ideas into a readable form. You're a great one!

The team at Moody Press is a joy and delight to work with. Greg Thornton, Bill Thrasher, Jim Bell, and Cheryl Dunlop have been invaluable partners and wonderful servants in helping me to put what is in my heart onto paper. Thank you for your confidence and commitment to me and to this book.

A special thanks to the Legacy team and to my Executive Assistant, Leonard Scott. This has been one of the busiest times of my life and ministry. Our staff members have been especially understanding and supportive in protecting my time and giving me the freedom to write.

My children, Bryan, Heather, Bryndan, and Holly, have provided the passion and motivation to preserve the timeless lessons I learned "at my father's knee." In a very real sense, they are the coauthors of this book.

My wife, Karen, is the visible display and definition of support. Her loving encouragement and willingness to sacrifice time with me not only to write but also to minister to others greatly humbles me. Sweetheart, I love you, and I do not deserve you!

INTRODUCTION

BRING THE
BLESSING HOME

On July 4, 1995, at 2:10 P.M., the greatest man I've ever known died. He was eighty-one years old and the grandson of a slave. He was my dad.

Who I am, how I love my family, and the choices I make in the daily course of my life have been profoundly influenced by my father. Not a day goes by that I don't think about him. His signature is all over my soul, and it is that signature I will write about in this book. For years I intended to write a book about the lessons I learned in life from my father. I wanted to have it completed and published while he was still living. However, the challenges of a growing family and ministry kept pushing this project into the background. I ran out of time, and Pop went home to be with the Lord.

Yet I believe that this was the way it was meant to be. Despite his boldness and strength, my father, paradoxically, was a very private person. He was a bit embarrassed by public recognition. He would much rather get the job done quietly than spend time talking about what he had done. He lived for his family and had an eye on the future. He wanted his children and grandchildren to be the visible display of who he was, how he lived, and what he believed, and he made the personal sacrifices to make that dream a reality.

This book is not a biography but a monument to one man's influence on succeeding generations. It's about character, strength, and, most important, hope. It's about picking up the mantle from those who have gone before us, embracing their success and not allowing their imperfections and failures to restrict our development, but rather to fuel our determination to do better.

Life is not determined so much by failures and successes as by our perspective on those failures and successes. Wherever we have God's gifts of perseverance and commitment, we have hope.

And we all do fail. Several years ago I had a less-than-delightful confrontation with our younger son, Bryndan. One morning, just before I took him and my older daughter, Heather, to school, I thought there was evidence beyond a shadow of a doubt that he had blatantly disobeyed me. I put the hammer down. I came down really hard on him that morning. After I had dropped him off at his school, my older daughter said to me, "Dad, you were absolutely wrong about Bryndan. In fact, he *didn't* do what you thought he did." She explained to me what had happened, and I realized that I was totally wrong.

I had to go and apologize to Bryndan. I took him out of his classroom to do it. When he came home after school that evening, I profusely apologized to him again. I confessed that I had made a judgment, but my judgment was wrong. I didn't have all the facts. I thought I knew what was right but, as his dad, I failed. I was wrong and I asked him to forgive me. He hugged me and said, "Dad, I forgive you."

So you're not hearing from any superhero of fatherhood as I write. Every father knows that there are times when we absolutely blow it. We're not God. We're certainly not perfect. Everybody tells us how we should be, how we should live, and what we ought to do, but we are still imperfect people. We have shortcomings. We have failures. We sin. We don't say things right. We don't do things right. We don't have adequate information. We make bad decisions. Again, it's not whether or not we will fail. We *will* fail; that's a given. Not only that: we're going to fail tragically at times. But the issue is what we do with those failures and bitter experiences. Our perspective on them is of great importance. Are we going to allow those experiences to be redemptive in our lives, even monuments of encouragement later on? Or are we going to allow those failures to permanently injure us and keep us and our family in that abyss of what is known as "dysfunction"?

When I was nineteen, I experienced a painful rite of passage. It almost drove a wedge between my father and me that could have fractured our relationship in such a way that it would have taken years to heal.

In many ways Pop and I are very much alike. We are both very determined (my wife says *stubborn* is a more accurate word), yet except for this instance we never really "locked horns." He gave me plenty of space while I was growing up and, frankly, I always clearly knew he was in charge. He didn't play power games with me or my two sisters. An attack on authority was handled quickly, clearly, and decisively.

But there came a showdown that was years in the making. Although Pop always encouraged and supported us in whatever we did, I felt a subtle expectation from him that I needed to fulfill a dream of his that was cut short by a coal mining accident. He wanted me to play baseball . . . and, perhaps, if I was fortunate, go all the way to the big leagues. I did play baseball and I was good. However, when I gave my life to Christ as a teenager and began to grow in my faith, my passion and fire for baseball died out. In its place would grow a burning desire to serve Christ. To walk away from the sport that had been the love of my dad's life and his dream for his son caused a bit of tension in our relationship.

The tension mounted when I went off to study at a Bible college. In all fairness, I don't think he was against my going into the ministry; he just did not have the assurance that I knew what I was getting into. In addition, that first year away at college I grew a sizable Afro, so my hair was very long. Now you have to understand, my father was a conservative kind of guy and he hadn't gotten into the long-hair style. He thought I looked like a wild man.

You get the picture: I have walked away from baseball. I have gone off to Bible college. And besides that, in his mind I have begun to look like the leader of some radical group.

It all came to a head on a weekend in March 1969. After classes ended Friday, I took the train home to visit my family. I had a great time with my mother, my uncle Henry, who lived with us, and my sister Elaina. I got a chance to spend some time with friends. All in all it was a good weekend. Except for Pop. The whole time he acted aloof and cool toward me. I managed to ignore it and not allow his "distance" to get to me.

That Sunday evening I needed a ride to the train station to catch the last train back to school. I went into the living room and asked Pop to give me a ride. His exact words were, "Boy, I'm not taking you anywhere with your hair looking like that." His response shocked me. I was stunned. Pop was always there for us. He lived his life for his family—this favor was no big deal; I was just asking him to take me a few miles down the road to the train station. This was completely out of character for him, and for a moment I was deeply hurt. Then I got very angry. I did something I had not done before and haven't done since. I raised my voice—no, I yelled—at my father.

Welling up within me was a bitter mixture of anger, hurt, and frustration. I did not sense the approval and blessing of the most important person in my life, my father. With my mother, sister, and uncle looking on, I told him that this had nothing to do with my hair but with the path I had chosen to follow. I told him that I was sorry for disappointing him by not pursuing baseball. I told him that I have to do what God tells me to do.

As I stormed out of the door (how's that for a mature, spiritual response?), I said I could make it on my own and I was not coming back home. My uncle caught up with me and took me to the train station.

When I realized what I had said to my father, I nearly had a heart attack. I was doubly surprised that he had taken it without responding, without saying a word.

A few weeks later, through the conviction of the Holy Spirit, common sense, and a tearful phone call from my mother, I went home to patch things up with my father. When we saw each other, we did not embrace tearfully or offer profound apologies. He simply said to me that I was free to be whatever I wanted to be. As he said those words, I heard a bit of fear in his voice. I felt the same fear. For we both realized how perilously close we had been to walking away from the incredible relationship we had enjoyed most of my growing-up years and from the really important issues in life that would frame and form a legacy.

That day our respect for each other was not only restored, but it was made stronger and deeper. Also, from that moment on Pop dealt with me more as a peer. He released me into manhood. I guess he realized that spring day that I was the important dream, not baseball, hairstyle, and choice of college. We both heard the wake-up call.

Conflict and bitter life experiences can be chances to

15

mature and to grow closer to others or excuses to stumble and drop out of the race. Crises present unique opportunities to decide the future for yourself and those around you. Judges chapter 11 tells a powerful story about Jephthah, a man who handled a bitter life experience and became a leader. I believe it's instructive to us. Look closely at these words in Judges 11:1–11:

> Now Jephthah the Gileadite was a valiant warrior, but he was the son of a harlot. And Gilead was the father of Jephthah. And Gilead's wife bore him sons; and when his wife's sons grew up, they drove Jephthah out and said to him, "You shall not have an inheritance in our father's house, for you are the son of another woman." So Jephthah fled from his brothers and lived in the land of Tob; and worthless fellows gathered themselves about Jephthah, and they went out with him.
>
> And it came about after a while that the sons of Ammon fought against Israel. And it happened when the sons of Ammon fought against Israel that the elders of Gilead went to get Jephthah from the land of Tob; and they said to Jephthah, "Come and be our chief that we may fight against the sons of Ammon." Then Jephthah said to the elders of Gilead, "Did you not hate me and drive me from my father's house? So why have you come to me now when you are in trouble?" And the elders of Gilead said to Jephthah, "For this reason we have now returned to you, that you may go with us and fight with the sons of Ammon and become head over all the inhabitants of Gilead." So Jephthah said to the elders of Gilead, "If you take me back to fight against the sons of Ammon and the Lord gives them up to me, will I become your head?" And the elders of Gilead said to Jephthah, "The Lord is witness between us; surely we will do as you have said." Then Jephthah went with the elders of Gilead, and the people made him head and chief over them; and Jephthah spoke all his words before the Lord at Mizpah.

This story is one of my favorites because it points out the redemptive nature of even some of our most bitter experiences. Jephthah was a product of disgrace and rejection. His mother was a prostitute; his half brothers rejected him. But his life in the wilderness of Tob prepared him for leadership. He only attracted misfits at first, but as time went by his own people called him home to take a position of leadership.

Here's the point: God redeemed the bitter experience of Jephthah's life to save a nation. You need to know that God can do the same with your bitter experiences to benefit your family. Don't despise those painful experiences. Don't hide them in the closet. You may not necessarily be able to talk about them, but allow those experiences that you've had—failure, great challenges, even danger to your life—to be a workout from which you draw strength to lead your family. The pain of your pilgrimage can bring ultimate healing to others. It can be a source for you to feed your loved ones spiritually, to feed them in terms of their character, to fuel their growth and development.

The tragedy of Jephthah's story is that his own family couldn't share in the joy of Israel's deliverance from the Ammonites. Jephthah's success came at a tragic cost at home. Let's pick up his story in Judges 11:29–36:

> Now the Spirit of the Lord came upon Jephthah, so that he passed through Gilead and Manasseh; then he passed through Mizpah of Gilead, and from Mizpah of Gilead he went on to the sons of Ammon. And Jephthah made a vow to the Lord and said, "If Thou wilt indeed give the sons of Ammon into my hand, then it shall be that whatever comes out of the doors of my house to meet me when I return in peace from the sons of Ammon, it shall be the Lord's, and I will offer it up as a burnt offering." So Jephthah crossed over to the sons of Ammon to fight against them; and the Lord gave them into his hand. And he struck them with a very

great slaughter from Aroer to the entrance of Minnith, twenty cities, and as far as Abel-keramim. So the sons of Ammon were subdued before the sons of Israel.

When Jephthah came to his house at Mizpah, behold, his daughter was coming out to meet him with tambourines and with dancing. Now she was his one and only child; besides her he had neither son nor daughter. And it came about when he saw her, that he tore his clothes and said, "Alas, my daughter! You have brought me very low, and you are among those who trouble me; for I have given my word to the Lord, and I cannot take it back." So she said to him, "My father, you have given your word to the Lord; do to me as you have said, since the Lord has avenged you of your enemies, the sons of Ammon."

The Ammonites were a stubborn foe, but nowhere in the story does God demand such a vow of sacrifice from Jephthah. Jephthah's vow demonstrated that he wanted success at any cost. Unfortunately, as it is for so many in our society, success came at a brutal cost to his family.

We need to do everything we can to make sure the benefits of God's redemption thrive in our homes, despite the hostilities and challenges we face day by day. Have you failed? Sure you have. Have you been defeated by challenges in your life? Absolutely. Have you been mistreated? Definitely. So have I. But sometimes I think we listen too much to the "victim talk" of our society. We accept where we are because of failures and problems in our lives. While we *do* need to accept failures, we do *not* need to allow them to keep us in a rut of victim mentality. Rather, we should look at failures and problems through the eyes of Calvary, through the eyes of a gracious, loving God who will help us to keep moving on in our lives. We all have those unsettling feelings that we're not doing enough.

I remember when we dropped our older son, Bryan, off at

college. I'd helped him move his stuff into his dorm room. Then we walked around and spent the day together. I was procrastinating to avoid the inevitable: saying good-bye. I realized as we stood there in the parking lot that this was it. Besides coming home for a few vacations, Bryan was basically going to be on his own. And I remember self-doubt just overwhelming me. My mind was racing ninety miles a minute: *Have I really done the job? Have I traveled too much? Was I there the times that he really needed me? This is it.*

As I got into my car for the drive home, I felt completely inadequate as a father. We all feel that way from time to time. Let's face it, the culture tells us in order to be a successful father you have to go to all the PTA meetings, you have to show up at all the Little League ball games, you have to be there at every soccer game, and you must keep your lawn manicured, your hedges trimmed, and your house painted. You have to always be around. When we don't meet these expectations, we feel as if we have failed. So what do we do then?

Let's start here: Never walk away. Show up when it really counts. I can give you a list of my dad's shortcomings. I could tell you a lot about his failures, but one of the great things about my father is that he never stopped growing. He was never afraid to admit he blew it. When he messed up, hurt our feelings, or whatever, Pop came back to make it right. We knew that we always had his heart. I can't tell you the number of times that that has influenced my role in my own family, my choices, my decisions about travel, and even my ministry direction.

In January 1982, I had scheduled a series of very important meetings in Chicago that were vital to the direction of our ministry. The morning I left for the Atlanta airport, I stood at the top of the stairs in our home, hugged my wife, Karen, and kissed our three children good-bye. Bryndan was a baby at the time, Heather was four years old, and Bryan was eight. It was raining and cold. The temperature was in the forties—miserable for Atlanta—and the forecast was not too promising. The rain was supposed to turn to freezing rain and then, perhaps, to snow. As I grabbed my bags and got ready to walk out the door, I turned around and said to Karen and the children, "I love you. If you need me, I'll be there."

Out of integrity comes your inheritance.

I went to the airport, got on the flight, and made it to Chicago. I conducted that evening's series of meetings. Early the next morning the phone rang. It was Karen. "How are you, honey? How's the weather?" I began.

"There are several inches of snow on the ground. Driving is really treacherous around here . . ."

"Do you have enough food? How about diapers?"

"Well, I haven't been able to get out." It was then I heard the fear in her voice. "Crawford, the furnace is turning off and on because of ice on the power lines."

"Do you want me to come home?"

"No. Don't come home. I know how important these meetings are for you." We went back and forth over the phone discussing whether or not I should go home. And although she said she wanted me to stay, I heard her heart. She wanted me to be there.

As I hung up the phone, a dear friend of mine asked, "Well, Crawford, is she all right?"

I said, "No, I don't think so. I have to go home because Karen really needs me there. Will you please chair the meeting today?"

I went to the airport and secured a flight back to Atlanta where, miracle of miracles, the airport was open. When I arrived home and opened the door—I'll never forget this—our older son, Bryan, saw me come into the house. He said to me with tears welling up in his eyes, "Dad, you said if we really needed you that you would be here."

That same son of mine, Bryan, is now preparing for the ministry. A few years ago, Bryan joined me on a radio talk show. Someone asked him, "How do you feel about your father traveling so much while you were growing up? Did you ever feel slighted?"

Bryan answered, "No, because we always knew that if we ever really needed Dad that he would be there for us." Then he told the story of that snowstorm.

You see, fellows, as men we need to make the most of the opportunities to impact our families. That's another strong, heartfelt motivation for me to write this book. I want to underscore again that we *will* fail and we *will* have struggles. Still, as you'll see through the progression of this book and the impact of my dad on my life, there are four things that are necessary in order for us to leave a legacy to succeeding generations. First of all, out of struggle met with a godly response comes strength. Second, out of strength comes discipline. Third, out of discipline comes integrity. Fourth, out of integrity comes your inheritance. I trust that these pages, as a tribute to my "leader of the band," Pop, will be a source of encouragement, strength, blessing, and hope for you as we get on with the task of shaping future generations.

PART ONE

OUT OF
STRUGGLE
COMES STRENGTH

CHAPTER ONE

SACRIFICE
THE RIGHT THING

"That's blood money."

My first car accident showed me how much I meant to my father. It was minor, a fender bender. I was on my way to my part-time job one morning. I thought the car beside me was turning right, so I moved into the right lane; when the driver continued going straight, he was unable to avoid hitting me. I called my father, afraid of his response because car insurance was high enough without an accident on my record. "Pop, I had an accident. It was my fault," I told him somewhat hesitantly.

"Boy, are you all right?" he asked. I heard the fear in his voice. I heard his heart connection to me. And I heard his relief when I told him I was OK.

Another incident that showed me my value in his eyes had actually happened years earlier, but it became a story he told often. When I was an active two-and-a-half-year-old boy, I fell out a third-story window. Whenever my dad repeated the story, telling me, "We thought we had lost you," I heard the sense of value he placed on my life. I knew that the loss of my life was a loss he could hardly imagine, and I knew how important I was to him.

I believe the greatest relational longing that a man has is the need for a "heart connection" with his father. When that connection is gone—whether it has been severed or was never established—it launches him into a passionate search for the love, approval, and affirmation of a dad. Men sometimes end up searching in the wrong place to fill that gap. Gangs, ambivalent feelings about their manhood, sexual conquests, anger, insecurity and uncertainty, the inability to establish wholesome relationships, and a host of other challenges batter their minds and threaten the emotional security of their lives without the "heart connection" with a father.

The tragedy, or the blessing, is that we tend to raise our children the way we were raised. More often than not we become the end result of what has been *done* to us more than of what has been *said* to us. If we grew up without a heart connection to our fathers, we'll battle a seemingly irresistible inclination to be disconnected from our children.

To our families, our presence is more important than anything else— including extra money.

We need God to connect our hearts to our children. Only He can break the cycle of distance and disconnection and empower us to begin a new legacy of love and tenderness bursting forth from our households. We can equip our children so that they don't have to long for the heart connection. They'll have it.

It's interesting that the very last verse in the Old Testament, Malachi 4:6, is a promise from God to "restore the hearts of the fathers to their children, and the hearts of the children to their fathers." Even though the primary application of this text has to do with God's dealing with the nation of Israel during the end times, we can't ignore the powerful application and implication for our families. God wants to, and can, reestablish the heart relationship between a father and his children. The word "restore" as used here suggests that other priorities have caused our hearts to drift from home. Time and attention have been given to other things, and those things, practically speaking, have become more important than our families.

We don't intend for this to happen. In fact, we often justify the shift in our attention by saying that we are doing these things in our families' best interests. Case in point: We work harder and longer hours to make more money so that we can improve "the lifestyle" of our families. Although we may improve their lifestyles, I wonder if we are improving their lives. *You* are the most important commodity to your children. For the promise to restore the hearts of the fathers to the children in Malachi 4:6 to be realized, as fathers we must understand the truth that, to our families, our presence is more important than anything else—including extra money.

A PRESENCE THAT CANNOT BE BOUGHT

Money cannot replace your presence. This message was permanently engraved on my heart at an early age. In fact, one of my earliest memories, from when I was four or five years old, demonstrates the value that my father placed on my sisters and me. For more than thirty years, my father worked nights for the A & P warehouse in Newark, New Jersey. I recall a discussion between my mother and father about whether or not he should work overtime during the holiday season. If Dad had worked on holidays he could have made triple time. Mom and Pop were talking about how nice that money would be. They could use it for a number of things to help their growing family.

As they were considering whether or not he should work on holidays, my father made a statement that I've never forgotten, although at the time I didn't fully understand what it meant. To my recollection he only said it one time, but it was one of those pivotal statements that forever let me know that his family was more important than anything else to Pop. He said to my mother, "Sylvia, that would be blood money because I've been away from these children too much lately." I felt valued. I felt significant in his life. It didn't make any difference to me as a little boy how much money we had or didn't have. I just knew that I had my dad. I knew that he was available. I knew that he cared about us. He was willing to say no to something that was evidently very, very important because we were most important. He made the decision that he would do without the extra money so that we could be with him and he could be with us.

As I think about this experience today, I find myself captivated by the expression "blood money." "Blood money" means sacrificing the core of your life for temporary financial gain. And Pop wasn't willing to do that. He was not willing to give up what was most important to buy something that was new, to have more trinkets and toys, to do more enjoyable things. We were his joy, not money.

CREATIVE FAMILY ACTIVITIES

To my knowledge, my father never read any articles or books on the family. He certainly didn't attend any family seminars that talked about the priority of home, but somewhere along the line he gained a commitment to the priority of home and his family. He never treated family matters like rocket science. He never sat down and lectured me about the intricacies of family relationships and the strategies behind being a dad and a husband. He just modeled it. You see, his priority was his family. He demonstrated this in many, many ways. Pop and Mom went out on dates regularly. She'd even get Pop to the theater every once in a while. That's kind of unbelievable when you know my dad's background, but Mom was a little bit "classier," and Pop would go along for the ride. My parents did things together. They spent time together as though they really enjoyed each other, which they did.

Every Saturday was family day. I remember, in the summertime especially, we'd go to an amusement park called Uncle Miltie's in Bayonne, New Jersey. Pop liked to play skeetball. We'd play that and go on the rides together. My dad was passionate about baseball. He loved the New York Yankees. Just about every weekend that the Yankees were in town, we spent Saturday in New York up in the stands, cheering them on. If they weren't playing, Pop would often take us to the drive-in movies on Saturday evening after spending the day at Uncle Miltie's. Pop just loved to hang out with us.

Pop made a big deal about birthdays. On our birthdays up through our teen years, Pop would take us to do whatever we wanted to do (within reason, of course). Some of my favorite memories stem from the fact that we celebrated our birthdays together, since my birthday is February 11 and his was February 13. We'd go over to New York City and have lunch or dinner together. Then usually we'd go see the New York Knicks play a basketball game.

I played Little League baseball and Pop worked nights. My games at the Boys Club on Littleton Avenue in Newark,

New Jersey, were after school, usually around 4:30. Even though Pop worked from 4:00 to midnight, he would always find out when my games were so he could swap some hours with a co-worker and be there at my ball games. He would stand there along the first base line and cheer me on. He was there.

So many times we'd just hang out together. Pop wasn't "into" shopping. Sometimes on Saturday mornings, when my mother and my sisters were going downtown to do some shopping, Pop would grab me and say, "Come on, boy, let's get out of here. Let's go for a ride somewhere." Maybe we'd drive to the park and play catch. Maybe he'd take me by one of his buddies' houses so I could just be there with him. It was no big deal, but I loved those times. To this day, I cherish the memories of those times when it was "me and Pop." Until I was twelve or thirteen years old, weekends weren't about being with my friends. I wanted to be with Pop, and he wanted to be with me. Even when I became a teenager, Pop remained an important part of my life.

He spent more time with me, his only son and his youngest child, than with the girls, but he loved to be with his daughters as well. Occasionally he took them shopping (that was the ultimate sacrifice to him), and he took them to New York on their birthdays. My sisters could really make his heart melt; I admit I admired the way they could, for all his toughness, get what they wanted by tapping into the tender side of him.

Although we were working-class people growing up in the central ward of Newark, New Jersey, we went on vacations together as a family every summer. We didn't stay in hotels; we visited relatives. Pop valued those times to give us special experiences together as a family and to expose us to a lot that was going on in the world. After we were all grown and had our own families, we used to sit around and talk with him about the old days. He often said with a smile, "You know, for a bunch of poor kids, you all sure experienced an awful lot." We'd smile, too, because that was eloquent. Our rich childhood stemmed from his commitment that we would experience life together as a family.

A FATHER'S AVAILABILITY

Availability. That's the key word: availability. Although Pop worked long hours and he wasn't home evenings during the week, we were confident that if we needed him he would drop everything to be with us. We somehow felt that he was always available to us. He spent the time that he had with us. His "blood money" statement represented his perspective on his family. Today many people emphasize that it's not just the amount of time, but the quality and the concentration of time with one's family that counts. That's true in many ways, but we fathers must also consider the access that we let our children have to us. Our children need to interact with us regularly and to know that at any moment, if they ever really need us, we will be there. Nothing in this world can take our place with them. Our actions and words must demonstrate that our kids occupy a special place and access to us that no one else except our spouse has.

Pop . . . was going to be a winner where it really mattered.

My father had a lot of friends. He was very respected in the neighborhood. There were guys at his job who consid-

31

ered him to be a good friend. He had plenty of opportunity to just "go hang out with the boys" if he wanted to, but I never recall my dad ever going anywhere I wasn't included. He never drank, he didn't go to certain places, and if I wasn't included he would simply pass on it. Here's the big point: Pop realized that he had a limited amount of time, so that meant that he had to make some sacrifices in order to effectively "pass the baton" to the next generation. I think we need to look at our lives from that perspective. All we have is twenty-four hours in a day, and once they're spent, they're gone. The Bible talks about our need to "redeem the time." My dad did that.

I sometimes look over all the things that are vying for my attention and I ask myself, *How in the world did Pop do that? How in the world did he find time to raise us?* And the answer comes screaming back: Pop just made up his mind that he was going to make some sacrifices and he was going to be a winner where it really mattered. No matter what happened in life, no matter what we kids might do, he was never going to give anyone reason to say that he did not give himself to his family. He was never going to be overwhelmed by guilt that he didn't give us the very best he could, namely himself.

LOOKING AT THE LEGACY

I'd just finished packing for a trip to Africa around midnight one evening in 1993 when I received a phone call from my mom. She said, "Son, your dad's in the hospital and it appears that he won't live." Needless to say, I canceled the trip and immediately flew up to my parents' home in Roanoke, Virginia. I went to my father's bedside along with my two sisters and my mother. Pop was conscious, but it looked pretty dismal. As he looked around and saw his family, the tears streamed down his cheeks. Pop simply said, "I did the very best I could." I knew exactly what he meant by that. I leaned over, kissed him on the forehead, and said, "Pop, you did a great job." You see, he gave himself to us. We're grateful to God that the Lord touched his body and he went on to live several years after that.

Pop's model and his "blood money" perspective hold me in check. They keep me accountable about how I spend my time with my family. When Karen and I got married, we thought it was a natural thing not only to spend time together on a regular basis, but also to have a vacation time. Then when the children started coming along, we instituted family nights and special family events. Birthdays around our place have always been special times of family celebration. As time has gone on, our kids and our ministry have both grown. There are greater demands on my time. I often reflect on the "blood money" perspective and the policy I've instituted in our office: If Karen or one of the children calls, no matter what meeting I'm in or who else I'm talking to on the telephone, I'm to be interrupted. I want my family to have access to my life.

Dad modeled several things before me. His example convinced me that there are only three things I do in life that nobody else can do for me. First, no one else can walk with God for me. I own that responsibility. Second, no one else can be the husband of Karen Loritts for me. I own that responsibility. Third, no one can be the dad of Bryan, Heather, Bryndan, and Holly for me. That I own. *Everything else that I do, somebody else can do.* In terms of ministry opportunities and leadership, somebody else can fill my shoes. But I must make sure that I'm not pursuing blood money rather than giving my heart to my family.

THE LEGACY PASSED

When Bryndan was eleven years old he wanted to play football. That fall I was scheduled to travel a great deal, but I made a commitment to him that I would be at all of his games. One weekend I was speaking on the West Coast on Friday, Bryndan had a game on Saturday, and I was scheduled to speak at a banquet in the Washington, D.C., area on Saturday night. In order to keep my word to Bryndan, I had to fly all night from Los Angeles back to Atlanta for his game. When I got there, rain was pouring down. There were only half a dozen parents in the stands. But there I was, in the stands with my umbrella up, rooting on this little guy of mine and his friends at their football game. Afterward Bryndan said to me, "Dad, I know you said you'd be at all my games, but you didn't have to come today. Nobody else was there."

I said, "Buddy, I promised you that I would be there, and I wanted to make sure that I showed up."

I just love hanging out with my children. I've had "dates" with my daughters from the time they were toddlers. I even have dates with my sons, although it's not really cool to call them "dates." We do things together. We spend time with each other. It's a part of my schedule.

Does it pay off? I was overwhelmed (and humbled) by a note I received from our older son, Bryan, a couple of years ago. Bryan was born on my birthday and we have done some very special things together on our shared birthday. His college career changed that. He was very busy on our birthday that year and I was traveling, and somehow we didn't communicate that day. But he wrote me this little note shortly after our birthday. It's a tribute to my dad as much as it is to me, and it shows how priorities and values are passed down from one generation to the next.

> Dad,
> Sorry this is late. I'm still trying to grasp the deep concept of responsibility. Maybe I wasn't taught, or didn't learn very well (ha ha!).

How's it feel to be 44 years old? I hope when I am 44 I can look back over my life and have the same sense of accomplishment that I know you must have. I need to pause here, though, to say "Thanks" for being a father in the true sense of the word. Somehow with all of your travels you managed to do more than live a balanced life and maintain a steady home. I do not feel shortchanged at all. I realize that some of my friends feel that way because their dads have been very, very busy, but I don't feel that I missed anything and for that I say thanks.

You are a model of consistency to me. A lot of times when I'm faced with decisions I'll try to imagine what you would do. You've given me the greatest gift a father could give a son: A legacy.

Happy belated birthday,
Bryan

Now I've made many, many mistakes. I know Bryan could probably write about those as well. Even here, Bryan does not mean that I've always been 100 percent consistent. I haven't. But I've tried to give my family my heart. I've tried to give them who I am. I've tried to communicate as much as possible because of Pop, a guy who played in the old Negro Leagues and worked in the coal mines, who labored for years at the A & P warehouse, who was not a community leader but certainly "did the deed" at home. I've tried to give my family some of the honey out of Pop's life, and it seems that God has honored him through my life to keep this thing going.

You can give your family the same gift.

Questions and Application

1. Many fathers are haunted by the idea that they're not working hard enough. But is there "blood money" in your life? Can

you think of something you can do without in exchange for more time with your family?

2. Dedicated time to each member of your family is important. When "dates" are mentioned in this chapter, the idea isn't an expensive time out, but dedicated time on your schedule. Set dates with your family members this week. Figure out with them how you can make these dates regular, scheduled events for both of you.

CHAPTER TWO

GUARD THE DEPOSIT

". . . he was the original *promise keeper."*

On June 26, 1995, I was ministering with Gary and Barbara Rosberg, some great friends of mine in Des Moines, Iowa. I had just finished speaking to some business and professional people there. When we returned to Gary and Barbara's home, a phone message was waiting for me. My mother had called. When I returned her call, she gave me a bit of dreaded news: She said that Pop was back in the hospital, and this time the doctor said that there was nothing more to be done for him. Apart from a miracle, they expected him to pass away in a matter of just a day or two.

My heart sank. Because of Pop's ongoing battle with congestive heart failure this was no surprise, but facing the finality of it was hard. I realized that if God did not intervene, very soon Pop would be in His presence. I caught the first available flight from Des Moines back to Atlanta, rushed home, returned to the Atlanta airport, and then flew to Roanoke, Virginia, that same day. My oldest sister met me at the Roanoke airport. We immediately went by our parents' apartment, picked up Mom, and headed to the hospital.

I was overwhelmed by what met me in that hospital room. Pop was lying in the bed with tubes all over the place. He went in and out of consciousness, barely recognizing the loved ones surrounding him. He was extremely tired after we prayed with him, so after a short time we went back home.

Once there, my mind went into another gear. Arrangements needed to be made for Pop's homegoing. This was probably God's appointed time for him to leave. I wanted to shield Mom from some of the burdens and pressures of details in preparation for Pop's death. Over the next few days I attended to some of their affairs between hospital visits. Things were just a blur, or so it seemed.

On June 29, the doctors released Pop from the hospital and returned him to the nursing home where he had been staying the previous two months. It was impossible to miss the debilitating toll Pop's battle to live had taken on his body as he arrived from the hospital. The ambulance attendants wheeled Pop into his room. He continued to drift in and out of consciousness.

I was scheduled to fly back to Atlanta to speak at a Promise Keepers men's conference. But as I stood with my mom and oldest sister around Pop's bed, I felt like I would be abandoning them. Worse, I felt that if I left for Atlanta I would be abandoning the man who always showed up in my life. When I turned to my mother while we were at Pop's bedside, I couldn't keep the emotions back. The tears began to flow freely down my cheeks; I didn't want to say good-bye. I said, "Mom, I'm calling to cancel the Promise Keepers date in Atlanta." I'd already told her that there would be more than seventy thousand men there, but as far as I was concerned, there could have been 5 million people there and my mind wouldn't change. I wasn't going to leave my mother, and I wasn't going to leave Pop because he never left us.

You have to understand that my mom is one of the sweetest, gentlest people in the world. She has not a confrontational bone in her body. But when I told her that I was going to cancel out of the Promise Keepers event, she turned to me with fire in her eyes and put her hand firmly on my arm. To this day her words ring in my soul. Mom looked in my eyes and said to me, "Boy, you get on that airplane and you go back to Atlanta because your daddy would want you to do it. You made a commitment and you do it. After all, he was the original promise keeper."

I thought, *Wow, this woman is tougher than I ever realized!* I looked at my watch. Time was running out for me to get to the airport. I read several portions of Scripture to my dad. I leaned over and told Pop how much I loved him and how much his life had meant to me and his family. I told him how proud I was of him and that he didn't have to worry about anything. I assured him that no matter what happened, I would make sure that Mom would be taken care of.

Then I kissed him good-bye.

THANKS FOR THE MEMORIES

Although it is only an hour's flight from Roanoke to Atlanta, that was the loneliest and longest flight I've ever taken. My heart was filled with competing emotions. Memories of great times together with Pop kept flashing across my mind. A flood of shared experiences and words overwhelmed me. I felt them as if they were happening right there at that very moment. Yet my heart was torn because we had to let Pop go. This was it. I thought about Pop's background, where he had come from and what made him the man that he was. Then I felt an incredible sense of responsibility and obligation to be a good steward of the legacy that he had given to my sisters and me.

In 2 Timothy 1:14, the apostle Paul wrote Timothy, his son in the faith, to give him a sobering charge and a clear priority: "Guard, through the Holy Spirit who dwells in us, the treasure which has been entrusted to you." Think about that phrase "the treasure which has been entrusted to you." I believe that in the context here, the "treasure" that Paul mentions is not simply the sum of Timothy's gifts, abilities, and opportunities. Earlier in the text, it's clear that Timothy's treasure is also in the legacy and the heritage that Timothy received from his mother and his grandmother. *All* those things form the treasure that Timothy is to guard as a living trust.

> *[Pop's life] made a statement that*
> *nothing was more important than home.*

My father gave us a treasure that had been passed down to him. As I flew back to Atlanta I began to think about the treasure that we had. As these thoughts and emotions were bombarding my soul on that flight back to Atlanta, I felt an overwhelming urge to pray. I wrote out my prayer to the Lord, and so poured out my heart to Him. Here is my letter to the Lord on that airplane:

Dear Father,

I feel so empty and somewhat numb; almost drained of my emotions. I am tired and sensing the loss of Pop, filled with the realization that he can leave us at any minute. Kissing him and saying good-bye broke my heart because this is the last time I will see him this side of Heaven. This is the end of the journey. We have done all that we can do.

Father, he is in Your hands. There is none like You. I ask You to take him sweetly and gently. Thank You for using the last three months to pry our fingers off of him. We have watched him suffer and deteriorate; his disorientation, his inability to walk, his loss of appetite, the fluid buildup, his difficulty breathing. Yet we have also watched him accept the inevitable. His acceptance of the nursing home, his words to the doctor still ring in my soul: "Whatever my son says, I will do." He never complained about the nursing home or the hospital. He just wanted to go home. I remember what he told us Monday night at the hospital. "In the morning I'm going to get up, wash up, put my clothes on, and go to church." Well, very shortly he will be in the greatest worship service he ever experienced.

Yesterday afternoon he told Elaina, "I have to say good-bye, I'm going home." These last few days he called for Mom, Elaina, Vonnie, and me. When I called him on Father's Day he asked me when I was coming to see him. Thank You, Father, for allowing me to see him before he died. He just wanted to be around his family. He's spending the last remaining hours of his life the way he has spent all of his life, thinking about and wanting to be with his family.

Thank You for the model he has been to me and to all of us. Thank You for hours of love and attention that we all received from him. The ball games, the drive-in movies, the vacations, the cookouts, the Saturday drives, the spankings, the incredible support. He was always there when we needed him. His family was his outlet. He spent his leisure time with us. He made a statement that nothing was more important than home. Thank You for the way he massaged our collar bones. Old Spice aftershave and deodorant will forever remind me of Pop. Footlong hot dogs, the Yankees and his homemade chowchow will, I'm sure, trigger a ton of memories.

Father, thank You for Pop. He's the greatest man I've ever known in many ways, especially as it relates to instilling in me and in us what it means to be committed to your family. Thank You for the supernatural way in which You have provided for his care. Thank You for allowing the house to sell and the closing to take place in January. Thank You for providing the funds through this to pay for his nursing home stay. Thank You for the apartment You provided for them and how inexpensive their moving costs were. Thank You for allowing him to be healthy enough to make the move and to see Your provision. Thank You that virtually all of their bills were paid. Thank You for the financial freedom this has given to Mom. Thank You for giving me the privilege of helping Mom with the finances. Thank You for allowing Elaina to be free to care for Mom and Pop these last few months. Thank You for Harold and Beck and Al, who have been a source of insurmountable strength and encouragement. Thank You for Vonnie and the trips that she has been able to make to visit them. To God be all the glory. Thank You for allowing me to read to him today. Psalm 57, verses 1 and 2, 5 and 7; probably the last passage he will hear this side of Heaven.

Something strange happened to me as I prayed that prayer. The sorrow was there, the sense of loss was present, but I was overwhelmed with praise to God for what He had done. I was also overwhelmed with praise to God for Pop's life, and there was a sense of joy in my heart that he was in God's hands. Not to get too dramatic here, but I felt a mantle dropping on my shoulders along with an awesome sense of responsibility I've carried ever since, that I'm to be a good steward of all that has been invested in me. I need to make sure that I take what has been given to me by a man who never had any recognition but quietly and simply "did the deed." I will take what his life represented and make sure that, with all that is within me, I multiply the influence of the principles Pop lived out every day of his life.

THANKS FOR THE FAITHFULNESS

A couple of days after that prayer, I found myself standing in the middle of the Georgia Dome speaking to more than seventy thousand men. The title of my message was "Raising the Standard for Our Children." I can't describe to you how distracted I felt. Just before I was being introduced, my assistant and my older son, Bryan, were with me behind stage on the cellular phone trying to get an update on Pop's condition. He was still around, but he was just barely holding on.

I didn't feel like preaching. There was a part of me that said I needed to be with my dad, but I wanted to honor my mother. I don't believe I delivered one of my better messages that day. I was there because of a responsibility. I didn't feel a special amount of liberty as I spoke, but God was gracious.

I spoke from Psalm 78:5–7:

> For He established a testimony in Jacob,
> And appointed a law in Israel,
> Which He commanded our fathers,
> That they should teach them to their children,
> That the generation to come might know,
>   even the children yet to be born,
> That they may arise and tell them to their children,
> That they should put their confidence in God,
> And not forget the works of God,
> But keep His commandments.

I talked about leaving a godly legacy through our families. Near the end, as I got ready to walk away, I had an overwhelming urge to tell the men the burden of my heart and to give my dad a tribute. As I did that the tears began to flow down my face, and it seemed as if a holy hush settled over the audience. I told them of my great love for Pop, and I told them of his heritage and legacy in my life.

"I almost did not come here to Promise Keepers because last week, while I was preaching in Iowa, I received a call from my mom that my dad was in the final stages of congestive heart failure—and that he wasn't going to make it," I said. "Needless to say, I canceled everything and flew to Roanoke, Virginia, where they live. Pop will probably die within the next couple of days. But I had to come back on Thursday; my mom said, 'Son, you go and do that Promise Keepers. Your daddy would want you to do that, because he was the original promise keeper.'

Because a slave taught his father
about the character of God
and the content of Scripture,
[Pop] molded my life.

"As I went there to the nursing home and said good-bye to Pop, I leaned over and kissed him and prayed with him, and said, 'Buddy, I'll see you on the other side.' I told him how much I loved him and I gave him a tribute for the wonderful job that he'd done. You see, my name is Crawford Wheeler Loritts, Jr. Both my boys have Crawford as their middle name; not in honor of me, but in honor of my dad. And I want to give you some hope tonight, fellows. My father worked for over thirty years in an A & P warehouse. He played professional baseball in the Negro Leagues. He's the grandson of a slave.

"My great-grandfather was a godly man. His name was Peter. He was a singing and praying man. He was illiterate, but he loved the Word of God, and he loved God with all his heart. He forged a generation of godly men.

"And despite the fact that I was born in the central ward of Newark, New Jersey, and that my dad never went to a family conference, and that he never went to a Promise Keepers, because a slave taught his father about the character of God and the content of Scripture, he molded my life. He finagled his schedule so he could be at my ball games. He provided for us. He did the very best that he could."

As I finished I felt somewhat awkward. I began to turn away, feeling a bit embarrassed because of the tears. Then an amazing thing happened. Those seventy thousand men leapt to their feet. Tears were flowing all over the Georgia Dome, and the ovation went on for several minutes. The ovation was not for me, because I wasn't particularly eloquent that day, believe me. The ovation was for a warehouse worker. The ovation was for a quiet man of character. It was for Pop. As I walked down, Bryan ran up to me and engulfed me in his arms because he, too, was so proud of Pop-Pop.

Perhaps now that he's in heaven, God will let Pop see the scene that took place that day.

Questions and Application

1. What are the three most important promises you can make —and keep—to benefit your family? Write them down, and keep them where you can refer to them often.

2. Carry a small notepad with you for one week. Whenever you make a promise to one of your family members, write it down. Review the list daily, and schedule the time to keep the promises you make.

CHAPTER THREE

MAKE IT HOME
BEFORE DARK

"You're never far from home."

At the end of every letter and phone conversation I have with Bryan and Heather, our two oldest children who are away in graduate school and college, I sign off with this statement: "Make it home before dark."

Of course, I don't literally mean to come in before the streetlights come on. It's a figure of speech. First, it's an affectionate statement reminding them that there is a place they can come to receive unconditional love and acceptance. If they ever feel like they're too far out on a limb, Karen and I will always be there for them. Second, it's a loving reminder for them to draw strength and direction from the values they were taught at home, especially when they face the challenges and temptations of life. Third, it is a reminder that they have come from somewhere and they are going somewhere.

I don't say "Make it home before dark" in an arrogant, controlling sense. We do not tell our nearly adult children what they should do with their lives. We want them to be, and to do, what God wants. Nonetheless, we want them to be good stewards of what has been invested in them and to cherish the gift that has been passed down to them from the time of Peter, my great-grandfather. I want them to grow up with the same security my dad gave to me and my sisters: No matter where you are, you are never far from home.

FOUNDER OF THE LEGACY

Peter, Pop's grandfather, was a slave. According to oral tradition, he was a slave on a Louisiana plantation and migrated with the family that owned him to what is now Catawba County, North Carolina. Our last name is probably taken from the family that owned Peter (the common practice in those days). Peter was an illiterate man. Since he couldn't read and couldn't write, someone probably spelled the name phonetically for him and it stuck. We are most likely directly related to anyone else who spells it L-o-r-i-t-t-s.

My father remembered Peter. He died when my dad was still a young boy, but Pop said that he could recall Peter rocking back and forth, singing and praying on the front porch of the old homestead in Conover, North Carolina. Most of the information that I've gathered about Peter has come from my dad and one of his oldest surviving sisters, my aunt Vera, who is our unofficial family historian.

Although he didn't have much in this world's goods, he was evidently a very generous man. Peter had acquired some land, and he gave the land for what is now Thomas Chapel AME Zion Church, which is across the street from the old homestead to this very day. There were two things about Peter that have forged the direction of our family for these generations. One is that Peter had a heart for God. He loved the Lord Jesus with all of his heart. Peter's singing and praying on the front porch were complemented by the passages of

Scripture he had committed to memory because he had his family members read those passages to him over and over again. The other thing that Peter had was a tenacious commitment to his family.

"You never walk away from home."

Peter had three children. The first was a son, H. P., who moved to Dayton, Ohio, and became a successful businessman and mortician. Then Peter had a daughter, Georgia, who married a man named Wheeler. They moved to Knoxville, Tennessee. Oddly enough, Georgia's husband was a mortician, too. Finally, my grandfather, Milton, remained in Conover to carry on the family tradition. Milton trusted Christ at an early age. He was a Sunday school superintendent and a friend of many, many preachers who "rode the circuit" to come and preach in Conover. Milton married my grandmother, Anner, and together they had fourteen children: seven boys and seven girls. My dad, Crawford, was the youngest of the boys. He was named after one of my grandfather's very dear friends, B. A. Crawford, who was a Methodist preacher. Pop's middle name was Wheeler after his aunt Georgia's husband.

KEEPER OF THE LEGACY

Granddad used to have the preachers come over to the house after their church services, usually about twice a month. My dad and my uncles used to tell stories about having to wait for their own meal until the adults ate. As they waited outside the dining room, they'd peek through the door to see how much chicken was left on the table. Pop said that one of the worst spankings he ever received was after he peeked through the dining room door to do his part in the "chicken update." The chicken was disappearing quickly that Sunday. Finally, the preacher finished it off, and my dad yelled out mournfully, "He ate the last piece of chicken!" Pop said that he suffered through a very bad spanking for that. That experience led to Pop's vow that, when he married and had a family, the children would eat with the adults at the same time they ate, guests or not. (And we did.)

I never met my grandfather. He died in 1947 before I was born, but my father, aunts, and uncles used to sit back and tell stories about him when they were together. From all accounts, Milton was a man of impeccable character and great integrity. I heard time and again that my father was so very much like him in terms of his perspective, character, and direction in life. My granddad was evidently a man of his word. So much of what Pop was came from him as well as from Peter.

Milton believed in hard work. He had acreage in Conover, so the family had chickens, some animals, and a garden. The kids had to feed and tend the animals. Everybody had something to do around the house; Granddad was a great believer that hard work was a virtue. Besides having acreage, my grandfather worked on the railroad. He would be gone for days at a time, but the center of his life was still his family. Some old sayings have been passed down from one generation to the next among the Loritts. One of them is "You never walk away from home," a philosophy that gave this book its title. Another is "You take care of your family first."

My dad grew up in an environment with the luxury of *not* having all the distractions we have today. His was an experience common to everyone who grew up in the early part of this century, from the 1910s through the Roaring Twenties and into the Great Depression: Lives revolved around family, church, and the immediate community, in that order. When Pop told stories of those days, he would talk openly of Jim Crow and segregation. Yet, ironically, he felt that families were closer back then because people realized quickly that nobody was going to take care of you *but* you. There weren't any "delivery systems" for assistance other than the church and the community.

> *Although there was a*
> *serious side about him,*
> *Pop was always fun to be around.*

Families helped other families. Just because there was no father in the household down the street, that didn't mean that a child would grow up without a male role model. People helped one another. Everyone had plenty of food on the table and kept a plate handy for somebody else. Adults even helped in the discipline of other people's children in their community. My dad was fond of recounting that if a kid got into trouble at school or in the community, if one of his adult neighbors found out about it, the adult not only had the right to correct the kid, but even to spank him. (Then when he arrived at home, of course, he was spanked again.)

The context of the culture brought out this sense of community. People realized that nobody else was going to take care of them; the only true friends they had were the Lord

Jesus and one another. My father and my mother both grew up with that perspective, so they had a profound sense of compassion and obligation to other people. To my dad's dying day, he felt it was everybody's responsibility to help those in need. If someone was in legitimate need, Pop felt it was his responsibility, if he could, to be a source of help and strength to that person. Mom and Pop grew up in an environment where the church really was at the center of the community. They worshiped together, they sang the praises of God together, and they lived as a community.

INHERITOR OF THE LEGACY

At a very early age, my dad trusted Christ as his personal Savior. He grew up in Conover "running rabbits in the open fields" (as he put it—he liked to chase them and, according to the legend, occasionally he caught one) and playing baseball with a passion. All of my aunts and uncles say that my father was the most mischievous one of them. He was full of energy, very athletic—and he would get into trouble. My mother didn't like for Pop to tell this to me, but he would tell me that he always counted the cost of his exploits. That meant if something was going to be worth the spanking in terms of the fun and pleasure that he would get out of it, Pop just went ahead and did it. He fully realized that he was going to "get it from the old man" or from his mother, but he'd go ahead and take those lumps. My father enjoyed life. Although there was a serious side about him, Pop was always fun to be around.

The Word of God and prayer were clear priorities in the Loritts household of Conover as my father grew up. My grandfather had a godly walk. He was committed to the church and was superintendent of the Sunday school. It was simply assumed that one's relationship with God would be the core of his life. The Loritts family assumed that family members would reverence God, live by the Word of God, obey it, and be in church.

Running Away from It All

Not everything is rosy in the story of my dad's life. All of our families have some kind of dysfunction associated with them. My dad was somewhat of a maverick as he grew up. I don't know exactly what happened; this is one of the incidents about which Pop never went into details. But I do know that my dad ran away from home when he was nine years old. Later in life, Pop mentioned that he was disciplined harshly for something that he did not do and that he was angry about it, so he ran away. Since there was a local circus coming through the area at the time of the incident, my father ran away with that circus. He ended up in Florida and stayed away from home until he was thirteen years old.

By the providence of God, an older woman in the circus took care of him. He made money performing at the circus and gave it to that woman. Finally, when Pop was thirteen, his father sent for him and he made things right at home, but he returned having missed four years of life at home. There was a reconnection there, obviously. My father only spoke with fondness concerning his siblings, his mother, and his father. We don't know what all took place while Pop was with the circus. To his dying day, he never talked about the details of his life between nine and thirteen years old. We all surmise that it was extremely painful because whenever we'd ask about it, Pop would change the subject or just shut down the conversation.

When Pop returned to Conover, he finished his schooling. He even went on to do two years of college at a place called Swift Memorial, which is no longer in existence.

Pop was an outstanding athlete. He played football, but the love of his sporting life was baseball. Pop played baseball with various bush league teams around North Carolina. The Negro Leagues were just starting to crank up. Pop tried out with a few teams, and he ended up playing with the Memphis (Tennessee) Cardinals. Some of his old cronies said they loved to see Pop play. He was fast, and he played a number of positions. His primary position was center field and, believe it or not, the last few years of his career he caught. Sometimes people glamorize the old Negro Leagues, but it was anything but glamorous back then. In the early years League players had to work other jobs, so in the off-season Pop worked in the coal mines in Dante, Virginia, and in Wheelright, Kentucky.

My Parents

My parents met in Dante, Virginia, after the 1940 baseball season when my mother went there to visit some relatives. They began to see each other shortly after they met. Even though they met in Virginia, my mother was from Lincolnton, North Carolina, just twenty-five miles from Pop's hometown of Conover. Their love for each other began to flourish. The relationship developed, and they were married on December 26, 1941.

You know the old saying that "opposites attract"? That couldn't have been more true for my parents. In fact, as I consider their personalities and dispositions and see how very different they were, it's amazing that they ever came together—yet they spent fifty-three years of their lives as husband and wife. They complemented each other so well. Sometimes I've heard people say that when a couple has been married for some time, the husband and wife begin to look alike. Although my parents didn't *look* anything alike and their personalities were totally different, they did begin to see things alike as the years unfolded.

My dad came from a very stable family background with both parents and a house full of kids. My mother never knew who her father was; my maternal grandmother was a single parent. My mother had a sister and a brother; my father had thirteen siblings. My father was the youngest boy; my mother was the oldest child. My dad was adventurous; he loved new experiences. He was also very matter-of-fact and "bottom line" when it came to people. My mother, on the other hand, is gentle, kind, sweet, and subtle—a very merciful lady. They were very, very different, but they grew into a common perspective.

We were never cold and we never went without food.

Shortly after they were married, there was a natural gas explosion in the Virginia coal mine where Pop was working. He lost an eye in that accident. That ended his baseball career in early 1942. Work was spotty and scarce then. Although Pop made a good living from the mines for that time, he felt like he needed to find a more stable situation. One of my mother's best hometown friends had moved with her husband to Newark, New Jersey, and reported that jobs were fairly plentiful there. She and her husband invited my father to come up and to see about getting some work. My dad went to Newark and settled into a job in a month or so. Then he sent for my mother, so in 1942 Crawford and Sylvia Loritts relocated to Newark. Pop had a couple of jobs before he landed the A & P warehouse job that was his employment for more than thirty years.

My sisters and I were born in Newark. My sister Elaina

was born January 29, 1946. Lavonia came along on April 29, 1947. Then Mom and Pop had me on February 11, 1950. (Pop wanted my mother to wait just another two days so I could be born on his birthday, but that was not to be.)

As soon as they moved to Newark, my parents joined the Trinity AME Zion Church. Both my mother and father became very active members. As they had been reared, the church was at the center of their lives and they made sure that core value was maintained in their own family.

My parents lived on Boston Street in the central ward of Newark when they first moved there from Virginia. They moved to 86 Wilsey Street shortly before they began having children. That's where my two sisters were born. When I came along they moved across the street to 83 Wilsey Street. We grew up in that community and enjoyed some great relationships with several families who lived there. For instance, we grew up calling our good neighbors Robert and Hattie Williams "Uncle Robert" and "Aunt Hattie" even though they were not related to us. My mother's lifelong friend who grew up with her in North Carolina lived around the corner with her husband; we called them "Aunt Lil" and "Uncle Coke." We grew up on Wilsey Street with plenty of love and plenty of people who watched out for one another. They took care of one another, just as they had in North Carolina where my parents grew up. My parents wanted to maintain and protect those rural roots and their deep-seated values.

My Family

We grew up in a household that was full of company. Pop always wanted to make sure that there was enough food around for company should they drop by, and we had plenty of people dropping by. My dad had a lot of friends who visited often. My sisters and I still talk with Mom about some of Pop's most deeply held values. Remember, Pop grew up in

the rural South in a family with fourteen kids. My grandfather, Milton, did everything he could to provide for them and I guess they had plenty. Nonetheless, Pop vowed from the time he was growing up that the two things he would always have for his family were, first, a warm house and second, plenty of food. Well, we were never cold and we never went without food. Pop made sure that the pantry was well stocked and we were well provided for.

Part of his motivation for a full pantry came from another value with which he had grown up: to help other people. Pop was continually helping neighbors in need, bringing them by the house for what they needed. We grew up watching that. My dad wasn't really outspoken in terms of his commitment to Jesus Christ. His was more of a quiet commitment that showed itself in the way he treated people—especially his neighbors—whether it was giving somebody some money if he had some extra money, offering a timely meal, or going to fix something for somebody else in the neighborhood. That's the kind of environment in which we grew up.

We had relatives who would send their children to live temporarily with "Uncle Crawford and Aunt Sylvia." Often Pop and Mom would help relatives find jobs and provide them with a place to stay free of charge until they got on their feet. In fact, my mother's brother, my uncle Henry, lived with us from the time I was born until the time I left for college. Henry and my father had an unusual and wonderful relationship. My dad worked nights and my uncle Henry worked days, so there was always a male influence in our household.

Going to Church

Just like his father and his grandfather did, Pop expected his family to be in church with him every Sunday morning. The rule in the house was that if we didn't go to church on

Sunday morning, we didn't go outside the rest of the day either. If we were too sick to go to church, then we were too sick to play outside. So church wasn't an option; we were expected to be there. We gave God the first day of the week.

Peter gave us a home.
He gave us a core.
He gave us a foundation.

Church was a family affair. We sat together as a family. We ate Sunday dinner as a family. Because my father worked nights, he was absent during the week at dinnertime, but even then we all ate together as a family: my uncle Henry, my mother, my two sisters, and me. There was no discussion or question about that. When we grew older and became more involved with various high school activities, we didn't always have the opportunity to sit down and eat together. But as younger kids, we did things as a family. It was a value of Pop's. He didn't get it from seminars or books or those kinds of things. He got it from his father. Where did his father get it from? Well, he got it from his father, Peter, who was a slave who had faith in Christ Jesus, a love for his family, and a desire to reach out and touch generations to come.

PETER'S LEGACY

I don't think a week goes by that I don't think about my great-grandfather, Peter. I never met him. We can't even find his grave when we visit the old cemetery behind the church in Conover, yet I sometimes believe that I stand on his shoulders. The blessings that I've received in ministry, the oppor-

tunities, the platform, the recognition; I believe all these things are due to that man's prayers setting the prayers of many others in motion.

I don't know what he prayed for as he sang and rocked back and forth on the front porch of the old homestead. I don't know what he saw down the road, but I know what he gave us. Peter gave us a home. He gave us a core. He gave us a foundation. And he gave us the security of knowing that no matter where we are in the world, we will never wander far from home. He established the Loritts address. Because of him, we have a place to come back to where we can lick our wounds and receive nourishment and strength. It is a launching pad that sends us forth in this generation and will send forth future generations. Core values are a treasure passed down from one generation to the next. Peter's touch was not only on Milton, H. P., and Georgia, but it has also been on succeeding generations. It's being realized even in the lives of our children.

TRACING THE LEGACY
BACKWARD AND FORWARD

Bryan, our older son, wrote a note not long ago that he gave to his younger brother, Bryndan. He told Bryndan how proud he was of him as he is growing up to embrace the values that I have passed down to them. As I read that note I thought, *From whom did I get those values?* I got them from Pop. Where did he get them from? His father, Milton. Where did Milton get them from? The slave, Peter. And the beat goes on.

As I'd go out as a child to play with my friends after dinner, one of my parents would remind me, "Boy, have a good time, but you know where the boundaries are. Don't go past West Market Street. Make sure that you make it home before dark."

It was great to grow up in a family that offered all the treasure of legacy mine did. It is a privilege to see that legacy flourish in my children. It is an honor to offer a heritage that they want to "come home" to in the midst of darkness.

And that's what your children are looking to you to provide for them.

Questions and Application

1. What are the positive aspects of the family heritage you received? What aspects are you working to make better for your children?

2. Take a few minutes today and jot down what you know of your own family history. For example: How many generations back can you trace? Do you know what your spiritual heritage is? Do you know details of your parents' courtship?

3. Take a few moments this week to tell your children a story about you from your childhood. It doesn't have to be an epic. Just talk to them about one aspect of what it was like for you growing up. Then make a habit of telling them stories about you.

PART TWO

OUT OF STRENGTH COMES DISCIPLINE

CHAPTER FOUR

LIVE
WISELY

"So you want to act the monkey."

Through years of ministry experience and travel, I've come to embrace the idea that every human being is brought into this world with two broad categories of emotional needs.

First, there is the categorical need for *nurture*. All of us have the need for physical and verbal affirmation. We need a tender touch. We need to be told that we are loved and that we are needed. We need to experience human warmth. If we don't receive it, we spend the rest of our lives starving for it. That hunger will take us places that we don't need to be.

But there's a second category that embraces the subject of this chapter. This broad category of emotional need is *accountability*. As odd as it may sound, all of us need daily doses of discipline and denial. We need to have boundaries and realize consequences. Those of us who never experience consequences end up self-destructing. We don't know what "no" means. When significant people in our lives who love us do not take a stand and tell us, "No, you're not going to do that" at critical points in our lives, we end up following the path of a fool.

Obviously the ideal environment for a child's growth is one balanced with both loving affirmation and accountability. All of that fits under the banner of love. My father believed that, as soon as possible, a child needed to know what was acceptable and unacceptable behavior and that consequences and discipline needed to be meted out as quickly as possible. This was not being cruel; this was setting the stage for balanced development in a life that would be lived with a sense of discipline and direction.

CHILDISHNESS OR FOOLISHNESS?

Pop had a saying whenever I did something that was downright foolish. He gave me a penetrating look and said, "So you want to act the monkey." He wasn't calling me an animal. It was just his way of saying, "Boy, you have better sense than that." He was pointing out that my behavior was totally out of sync with what I knew was right. The behavior may have been funny and entertaining, much like a monkey at a carnival sideshow, but it was making me look terribly foolish and silly. The principle was simple: You can't live your life based upon silliness.

When I was in the fifth grade, I brought home a report card that was outstanding on the academic side but absolutely dismal on the conduct side. There were huge U's (meaning totally unsatisfactory) written down in every area in which my teacher evaluated my conduct. My problem was that I never missed an opportunity to have fun in class. I would get my work done quickly and in good order. Because I often finished before others, I would become "creative" with my time. Usually that meant some mischievous activity.

Well, when I brought this report card home and showed

it to Mom, she just shook her head. My fifth-grade teacher, Mrs. Codner, had gone to the trouble to write on the card itself that I was "making great progress in becoming the class clown." My mother was upset at that. To my utter distress, my dad was home right then. (He had every Saturday off and then he would rotate one evening during the week to be home.) My mother immediately gave the card to my father and he looked at it, read the comment, and then made his "monkey statement" with an extra line: "So you want to act the monkey, huh? Well, I know how to make monkeys dance." Without going into much detail, let's just say that Pop kept his word, and that evening I gave up my ambition of being the class clown.

> *People become fools when*
> *their foolishness is not checked.*

What makes that whole experience stick out in my mind is the fact that my father once again drew a line in the sand and said, "No, buddy, you're not going to act like this. You know better than this and I'm not going to let you act this way." You see, Pop understood that if I continued to act that way, I was going to become a fool. Consistent foolishness produces fools. My father understood that it was a dangerous thing to let a child's foolishness go unchecked. When Pop read that report card, he could have chuckled and said, "Well, Sylvia, boys will be boys. Look at his grades, he's doing well in school. What he's doing is not destructive; he's just being a little bit of a class clown." But Pop knew my behavior was not acceptable. I was at an age where I needed to dial down and stop the "class clowning." Pop was going to put a stop to it.

Although it is inappropriate at times to joke around and to engage in some horseplay, there is a time and a place for it. It's just that my father felt that Mrs. Codner's class was neither the time nor the place for it. A major part of maturity is understanding what is appropriate behavior for various situations. People become fools when their foolishness is not checked. For example, it is not cute when our children initiate destructive behavior. Continued foolishness will diminish your child's potential. We've all met people who have incredible intellects and great abilities but who, through a series of undisciplined and unchecked choices in their lives, have never reached their full potential. If their foolishness goes unchecked, at the end of life their legacy will include a long list of regrets: "I should have, I could have—but I didn't."

The core of a fool is a rebellious heart.

My father knew that for my sake he could not let me do whatever I *wanted* to do, or else I would never be able to do what I *needed* to do (and, ultimately, really wanted to do). There is great freedom in self-denial. Pop knew that the more I practiced saying no to my foolish impulses and inclinations, the better I would be able to say yes to the right things in life. Again, I'm not suggesting that occasional foolishness will make a person a fool. However, a pattern of consistent foolishness will deeply entrench foolishness in one's character.

DEFINITION OF A FOOL

That brings me to what I consider to be the definition of a fool: *A fool is a person who refuses to live and to behave in light of what he knows is right and becomes a willing slave of his impulses.* Fools have willfully chosen to reject what they know is right to do. Instead, they live by what feels good and what is expedient.

Fools destroy themselves and everybody who comes in contact with them. They're not just content to exercise their own foolishness. Because they have willfully chosen to reject what they know is right, they want other people to join them in their foolishness.

Fools can be very subtle people. Sometimes we think that fools are just outright ridiculous and unrighteous. Indeed, the core of a fool is a rebellious heart. Through willful choices the person has decided to reject what is right. But in my years of ministry, I've met a number of Christians who are fools. Believe me, there is no worse fool in the world than a biblically accurate, informed fool. These people know and embrace truth intellectually, but they manipulate truth to camouflage a heart that is not willing to do what is right. They don't want to repent of wrong in their lives. They don't want to do what is right. There is a damaging element about their direction because they do not desire to live transparent, responsible lives in every detail. They don't want to face up to their biblical and moral obligations in terms of their lifestyle.

Fools want to justify their rebellion and pull other people into their foolishness. A telltale sign of a fool is when a person is confronted with obvious truth—particularly as it relates to his behavior—and refuses to change in response to that truth. I've seen churches, ministries, Christian institutions, families, and marriages sabotaged and destroyed through the activity of a sophisticated fool.

FORMING A FOOL

The tragedy is that fools are formed in early childhood. I don't think my father necessarily processed it this way, but he had a sixth sense that I was getting a little bit too old to aspire to be a class clown. My "acting the monkey" was too much of a behavioral pattern, and it needed to stop for my own good.

Children need to be taught that foolishness has consequences.

The book of Proverbs has some sobering things to say about fools and foolishness. Look at Proverbs 10:1: "A wise son makes a father glad, but a foolish son is a grief to his mother." Check out Proverbs 17:25: "A foolish son is a grief to his father, and bitterness to her who bore him." Examine Proverbs 19:3: "The foolishness of man subverts his way, and his heart rages against the Lord." Continue to the first part of verse 13 of Proverbs 19: "A foolish son is destruction to his father." Then consider this solemn warning in Proverbs 19:18: "Discipline your son while there is hope, and do not desire his death." I believe the point of Proverbs 19:18 is to encourage parents to carve out the foolishness in their children before it is entrenched in their characters. Take care of it.

Consequences and accountability are crucial tools in driving foolishness out of a child. Allowing children to ignore their foolishness and destructive behavior—even in the name of "love"—by constantly bailing them out of situations their own irresponsibility has caused only encourages them in their foolish behavior.

DRIVING FOOLISHNESS AWAY

One way to be sure kids do not grow up to be fools is by training them in habits of responsibility from their early years. My dad really believed in letting us, as soon as possible, own the responsibility of handling money. Consequently, we received an allowance. When I was a kid coming along, I worked part-time, but for several years Pop even supplemented that income with an allowance. He made this statement every Saturday when he handed out our allowances: "You need to learn the value of a dollar. Now look, this is your allowance. When it's gone, it's gone. Don't come back *here* when it's gone." In other words, we could throw it away, we could spend it on whatever we wanted to spend it on, but if we wanted to go to the movies during the latter part of the week, or if we wanted to buy a soda, or if we wanted to buy an ice-cream cone, we had received the money to make that happen the previous Saturday. If we ran out of allowance too soon, we just watched the others enjoy theirs. That taught me early and quickly about handling money. Trust me, Pop would *not* bail us out on that. That way we learned that money didn't flow like water.

Whether the issue is handling money or behaving responsibly, children need to be taught that foolishness has consequences. Our younger son has a friend we'll call "Billy" (that's not his real name) whose parents rarely, if ever, made him face the heat of the consequences of some of his foolish behavior in grade school and in middle school. Billy is a very talented athlete who played Little League baseball with Bryn-dan. In fact, he is outstanding in his ability to play ball. It's just that his unrestrained foolishness is destroying him. Now that Billy is in high school he is heading down a path that, apart from supernatural intervention, will either lead him to the morgue or to prison.

This is an area where we as fathers need to shine. This is where we must make the necessary sacrifices to be involved in the lives of our kids to keep check on their behavior. We must make sure they know there are boundaries, that they understand well that not everything is going to go. You don't have to be an ogre to make the point. We knew that Pop loved us because he laughed and joked with us. That very fact made it easier for us to take the boundaries from him.

That's what our kids need from us. We need to be there with them and be involved with their lives so, as we see these patterns emerging, they don't get out of hand. We can't afford to be so busy with our own lives that our daughter Shantai ends up at a counselor's office in the school, or our son John-ny is so out of control that we have to go to the police station when the patterns of a fool have emerged in his life. I'm not saying that our kids are perfect. None of them are. We can do all of the right things and some of our children will still turn out to be less than we hope. Even the best of our children embrace some foolish behavior at some time. Regardless, let's make sure that we are doing all that we can to avoid giving them any parental justification for their foolishness.

TEENAGE FOOLS

One of the most difficult times to deal with foolishness in the hearts of our kids is when they get into those "know-it-all" teenage years. You know what I mean: that age between twelve and seventeen when all of a sudden they know every-thing that there is to know about their lives, what they ought to do, and what they ought to be. So they lovingly (and sometimes not so lovingly) ask you to take a little "parental parenthesis" and step back from them.

> *"Experience . . . is the only
> school a fool will attend."*

My son Bryan gave me permission to tell this. When he was about fifteen years old, he began collecting caps from different professional sports teams, especially from the NFL. When I would travel to one of the NFL cities, I made sure that I brought him back a cap from the local franchise. I was in San Francisco one weekend when Bryan had all of the NFL caps except the one for the 49ers. Need I say that one of my assignments while in San Francisco was to get that cap for him? Unfortunately, I forgot about that mission until I was at the airport on my way back out of town. If you've ever shopped at the airport, you realize how expensive things are there. I went into the airport shop, found the cap, and thought, *Oh, I shouldn't pay this much. Then again, I promised Bryan.* So I went ahead and bought the cap for sixteen dollars and took it home. Bryan was delighted to get the cap.

Bryan had informed me earlier that, in his high school, some of the guys were stealing team caps from the other students. So as I gave Bryan the 49ers cap, I told him, "Now, Bryan, if I were you I wouldn't wear this cap to school. I'd just keep this cap here on the mantel. You have other caps you can wear to school."

Bryan responded, "I know, Dad. I'll take care of it. Don't worry, I'll take care of it."

I said, "OK, buddy, fine. Just remember I bought this cap and it wasn't exactly cheap." That ended the discussion.

I don't know what possessed me, but after a few days I asked Bryan, "Well, Son, where is your 49ers cap?" He began to stammer and make excuses and speak around the issue. I looked at him, smiled, and said, "Somebody took that cap, didn't they?"

Bryan was caught. He said, "Yeah, they did. But, Dad, I know who it is and if you come to the school, I think we can get it back." I knew he loved that cap. I was about to go to the school and get it. Because I paid for the cap, it was my money that thief had stolen.

But as Karen and I discussed the situation, I decided against taking action. He really loved that cap, but Bryan needed to learn a lesson. I told him, "Bryan, I told you not to take that cap to school. You were bent on taking it anyway, and I'm not going to replace it. This is a lesson to you. Embrace it." Then I offered him one of my favorite lines that I had used with my children many, many times before: "Experience is not always the best teacher, but it is the only school a fool will attend."

Bryan is an extremely responsible young man. In fact, when he was a little guy, just two or three years old, I'd take him with me when I went to preach someplace, and I wouldn't even have to take him to the nursery. I could put Bryan on the front row with some coloring books or a picture book and tell him, "Son, don't get up." Bryan would sit there and be still. He has always handled his money and affairs wisely and we're very, very proud of him. But along the path he has had to learn some lessons just like all of us do. He's had some experiences that, shall we say, caused him to internalize wisdom.

Bryan went to college in Philadelphia. We live in Atlanta, more than seven hundred miles away from the City of Brotherly Love. Bryan drove an older car. It was in pretty good shape, but because of the mileage and wear and tear on the vehicle, his mother and I were both concerned. We decided we'd feel a lot better if Bryan had a credit card to help with some emergencies just in case something happened to the car. So I gave Bryan a credit card, on my account, with his name on it. I instructed him, "Son, don't ever use this card without calling for my permission first. If there's an absolute emergency with the car, then, of course, you do what you need to do and we'll work it out." We never had any problem with it during Bryan's first couple of years in college. He always called Karen or me to tell us what the situation was and then to receive permission to use the card. We paid the bills in those situations and were just glad to know he was safe.

One day as I was looking over statements from that particular credit card, I noticed several purchases under his card number that we knew nothing about. It caused me some concern; I thought somebody had stolen the card and gone out on a shopping spree.

I quickly called my son and said, "Bryan, did you lose that card or something? I'm looking at your card statement here and I see some purchases at some clothing stores that Mom and I know nothing about. What's happened?"

I expected he would say that he had lost the card or that it had been stolen. There was a little bit of silence on the other end of the phone before Bryan said to me, "Dad, I'm sorry. I was out shopping with some of my friends and I don't know what got into me. I wanted some things; I really didn't need them, but I decided to buy them."

I replied, "Well, Bryan, you know that's a little bit out of character for you. Why didn't you ask, if you needed something?" I started to let it go but then, as a matter of principle, I thought, *No, don't let this go. Have him pay you for it.*

This was just before the Christmas break. Bryan was coming home for the holidays. When he came home, I said, "Son, I want you to give me the money for what you spent." It wasn't a whole lot of money but it was significant to him. He was a college student, remember; he worked part-time, but he needed every dime that he had. Still, this was an important lesson. Bryan was sincerely sorry. He apologized profusely, saying, "Dad, it was a very foolish thing that I did and I'll give you the money; I'll pay you." There was never any argument with him. True to his word, he gave me the money at the beginning of his Christmas break.

Karen and I had already determined what we'd do with Bryan's money. After the holidays, just before he was getting ready to go back to school, I took Bryan out to lunch and told him, "Son, you know how proud I am of you. Mom and I love you. We know that you are very responsible and I thank you for giving us this money." Then I reached into my pocket and said, "But I want to give it back to you because you showed me something. You owned up to what you did. You demonstrated to me that you understand this was a foolish thing to do, but you were willing to make it right. I want to give this back to you and I hope that you learned your lesson."

He didn't want to take the money back. "No, Dad, I was wrong. I want you to have the money."

I replied, "No, I want to give it back to you. That's grace."

You know, God deals with us in grace. Even when we talk about accountability and consequences with our children, we have to be gracious. We have to let them pay the consequences for their behavior, but we also have to ask God to give us insight to know what the balance is between consequences and grace.

And that's wisdom, a commodity desperately needed to keep another generation from taking the path of fools.

Questions and Application

1. Take a moment with your spouse this week to talk over the procedure of disciplining your children. Do your kids understand that some actions will have unfavorable consequences? Do you spend enough time with them so they can receive boundaries from you?

2. What are some behaviors in your children that concern you? Have you taken the time to talk with them about their behavior and how it might benefit them in the long run to change?

3. List three things each of your children do consistently that make you proud. Be sure you include character traits, not just talents. Tell them about those things today.

CHAPTER FIVE

SHOW UP

"You never walk away from responsibility."

The words "responsibility" and "obligation" are almost profane in our culture today. It's as if, *en masse,* we have lost our sense of commitment and the will to do anything difficult, anything we dislike, or anything we simply don't want to do. Sadly, our feelings determine what we do, how much we do, and how long we do it.

Somewhere along the line we have bought the myth that the goals of life are happiness and personal fulfillment. Therefore, if ever we find ourselves in a place where we feel less than happy or fulfilled, we think we have to change our address. In truth, real fulfillment is the by-product of obedience and faithfulness. It is the completion of the assignment that brings deep joy.

Life should be lived intentionally. Fulfillment and purpose are not the product of broken commitments and promises and a string of abandoned responsibilities. Depth of character, self-esteem, and, ultimately, fulfillment come from the satisfaction of rising to the challenge of your commitments. This provides the backdrop in motivation for perseverance and faithfulness.

In Luke 19, Jesus told a powerful story about faithfulness regarding the use of money. Verses 12–13 begin the story:

> A certain nobleman went to a distant country to receive a kingdom for himself, and then return. And he called ten of his slaves, and gave them ten minas, and said to them, "Do business with this until I come back."

When the nobleman came back, he called the servants to ask for their accounts regarding how much profit they had made with his money. The first slave had earned ten minas, and the master gave him authority over ten cities. The second slave had earned five minas, and the master gave him authority over five cities. Each of the slaves reported similar earnings. But then one of his slaves came with a different report. Luke 19:20–26 tells the rest of the story.

> And another came, saying, "Master, behold your mina, which I kept put away in a handkerchief; for I was afraid of you, because you are an exacting man; you take up what you did not lay down, and reap what you did not sow."
>
> He said to him, "By your own words I will judge you, you worthless slave. Did you know that I am an exacting man, taking up what I did not lay down, and reaping what I did not sow? Then why did you not put the money in the bank, and having come, I would have collected it with interest?"
>
> And he said to the bystanders, "Take the mina away from him, and give it to the one who has the ten minas." And they said to him, "Master, he has ten minas already." I tell you, that to everyone who has shall more be given, but from the one who does not have, even what he does have shall be taken away.

Let's review the details. Jesus recounted that a very wealthy nobleman was preparing to take a trip to a distant country. The nobleman called together ten of his servants and gave them some money to invest while he was away on his journey. When the nobleman came back, he received a report concerning the results his servants had achieved. All but one of them had a good report to offer. All but one had "done business" with the money and come back with a profit.

But the last servant didn't do anything with the money. He just took it and hid it in a piece of cloth. Evidently he was lazy. Not only was he lazy, but he also lied when it came his turn to give his report. In essence, the servant said, "Master, I knew you'd call me to account for this money. That's why I knew you'd be pleased when I hid it"—when in fact the nobleman had made his investment expectations quite clear from the outset.

Pop kept his sight on what needed to take place.

The nobleman expected his servants to "do business" with the resources he had given them, to conduct themselves so they would have more in the end than they had when they began. Those who responded in obedience were rewarded. The one who didn't lost it all. In context, Jesus is teaching that when you are faithful with what has been given to you, you will receive more. The converse is also true: When you are not faithful with what you are given, opportunities will elude you and even be taken away from you. I believe that this indeed is the perspective and "formula," if you will, for joy and fulfillment in life.

LOYALTY AND COMMITMENT

So what are we doing with the families that God has given us? Are we investing in them or ignoring them?

My parents were married for more than fifty-three years when my father died. When I look back and think of my childhood, I'm amazed at my father's incredible consistency and faithfulness. I never once heard him complain about having to go to work to put food on the table and provide for our needs. Day in and day out, Pop would get up, drive to work, and be there on time (usually ahead of time). He'd work hard, come home, and share the fruits of his labor with his family. He considered it a privilege to do it.

> *Pop thought that work and integrity went hand in hand.*

I'm sure there were days when Pop didn't feel like working. I'm sure there were times when he could have said, "What's the use? This is too hard." Yet Pop realized that he had made a vow to his wife on December 26, 1941, to love, cherish, and take care of her. He had made a commitment to his children that he would provide a roof over their heads and the essentials of life. So, with that sense of obligation and responsibility, he would get up, go to work, and provide for his family. He did it with a great deal of joy. In fact, Pop's ability to provide for us was one of the things he took great pride in after he retired. When we would visit Pop loved telling the stories of all his working years and being able to meet the needs of his family.

Although the end result brought him great joy, I'm sure there was a lot of pain in the process. But Pop kept his sight on what needed to take place. He knew he was responsible to bring us to maturity and to meet our needs until we could take care of ourselves—and that meant teaching us the same kind of responsibility that he practiced. Whenever I didn't want to do something around the house, or if I had a responsibility that I just "let drop," my father would grab me, look me straight in the eye, and say, "*You never walk away from responsibility. If you've got a job, you do it.*"

I've never forgotten that. It rings in my mind today. To Pop, loyalty and commitment were two important building blocks in a person's character. He felt that a person must finish what he was supposed to do before he did anything else. We completed our work first and *then* we played. Saturday mornings, especially, were work times around the house. If we wanted to do something later in the day, we did our work first. Then our work was inspected by either Pop or Mom. If it passed inspection, we were free to do what we wanted to do later on. That taught us that everyone who lived in the Loritts home had responsibilities. Work was not something to be avoided; it was a part of life.

INTEGRITY AND WORK

Work and responsibility were important issues to my father. I believe Pop thought that work and integrity went hand in hand. Pop taught us to be responsible through work. Whether it was a classroom assignment or cleaning something around the house, we were learning about obligation, duty, and responsibility. Pop said to me time and time again when I complained about a task before me, "Well, boy, you're going to have a wife, you're going to have some kids, and you are going to have to bring home the bacon. So you've got to learn to do it right now."

He never made a promise to us that he did not keep.

Pop felt that there was a sense of wholeness related to a good, honest day's work. The principle that he underscored in our lives was this: Not only is it honorable to be counted on, but it is a person's duty to do both what he says he is going to do and what he is supposed to do. Pop was teaching me the importance of "showing up." He felt that if a person said he was going to do something, he should expect to have others expect him to do it. Pop would often remind me, "Son, you know the only thing you have as a man is what you say. If you don't do what you say, then you don't have much else." A person's word was a very important issue to Pop, so if someone didn't do what he was expected to do, he had to have an awfully good excuse for not following through.

The expectation to follow through even extended to our part-time jobs outside the home. We were not allowed to simply quit a job. When I was sixteen years old, I began selling shoes at a local shoe store. If I ever complained that it was hard, or I just didn't like something and I wanted to quit, Pop said, "No, you're not going to quit unless you're being grossly mistreated or there is some insurmountable situation." As Pop saw it, not liking something was never a good reason to walk away from anything. Pop would say, "There are a lot of things in life that I don't like. But if you walk away from things that you don't like, you'll be walking away for the rest of your life."

Don't get me wrong; Pop was not "all work and no play." He certainly didn't run his home like a concentration camp. Pop was a blast to be around; he had an incredible sense of humor. Still, he had very strong boundaries. He had a clear sense of priorities, and his sense of personal responsibility was nonnegotiable. He felt that every person had the responsibility of doing the very best he could with what he had. Again, in his way of thinking, owning responsibility was proof that an individual was an honorable, trustworthy person. There was a direct relationship in Pop's mind between one's ability to follow through on a responsibility and that person's truthfulness. That's the reason he never made a promise to us that he did not keep.

I know that sounds like an incredible statement to make—almost unbelievable—but it really is true. (I also have to say that, regrettably, I've made promises to my kids or to family members that I was not able to keep.) Allow me to balance that statement by saying that Pop made some promises that he couldn't immediately keep. Sometimes circumstances would come up and he couldn't follow through in the time frame he thought he could. But Pop would never just drop a promise. For example, if he promised to take me to a ball game and he couldn't do it, he would simply say, "Son, something else has come up. Let's reschedule it." And he would. The fulfillment of the promise might be delayed, but Pop never did make a promise that he would not keep. I can still hear his words ringing in my head: "Boy, do what you say you're going to do." To him a person's word was more important than his comfort. Feelings at certain points in our lives were irrelevant, especially when it had to do with fulfilling a commitment.

KEEPING COMMITMENTS

This perspective has greatly influenced my outlook on life and the way Karen and I raise our children. When our older daughter, Heather, was a junior in high school she played in the high school band. She had a lot going on that year; in fact, her schedule was packed too full. By the middle of the year, Heather wanted to quit the band. Karen and I both said to her, "Sweetheart, we're not going to let you quit the band in the middle of the year. We're sure there are many other people there who play the flute, and perhaps in your way of thinking they won't even miss you. But you gave your word to the band director that you'd be in the band this year, so we're not going to let you quit." And my oft-quoted line to her followed: "If you quit now, you might develop a pattern of quitting whenever you don't like something, or when something becomes tough."

Our boys, too, have been through this. Both of them are athletic. They enjoy sports. But we remind them at the beginning of every season that if they go out for any sport and they make a team, "if you play, you stay." Whether he gets playing time or not, he doesn't quit. If he's on the team, even if he is sitting on the bench, he stays on that bench until the ride is over because it is important to learn "bench lessons" in life too. It's not about just playing a baseball game (or basketball game or football game), it's all about developing perseverance and faithfulness. It's about being a man of your word and enduring until the end.

When our younger son, Bryndan, played Little League baseball, during one summer he had the opportunity to play on the Atlanta team that played in the Little League World Series. When the summer was over, the team wanted him to play with them the next summer. When he heard about it, he was really excited. (So were Karen and I.) Bryndan has great ability in baseball; he is an outstanding player. But there was a hitch in Bryndan's opportunity that bothered me: Long before the opportunity with the LLWS team came up, Bryndan had already given the coach of his neighborhood team his word (and so had I) that he would be playing with his team that summer.

Perseverance is really the foundation of anything that takes place in life.

This was a dilemma; if Bryndan played on the LLWS team, the skill level, exposure, and number of games would really contribute to his development. Yet, as we thought about it, prayed about it, and discussed it with Bryndan, I concluded that his word meant more than taking advantage of a great opportunity. I told him, "Son, I'm not going to let you do that. I want you to be a man of your word. We promised our neighborhood coach that you would be on his team this year. If God wants you to play baseball on a team like the other one, then He'll give you that opportunity without you having to give up your integrity or honesty in the process. It's important that you learn how to keep your word. This is a test, and I want you to grow up to be a man who is honorable and will not walk away from what you say you'll do."

Years later, when Bryndan was in high school, he tried out for the basketball team. He was never as good at basketball as he had been at baseball, and the team seemed to be made up of players with greater basketball skill than my son showed. So, quite frankly, I was surprised when he made the team. Later I asked his coach what made the difference. He told me he had been impressed by Bryndan's character—his faithfulness, reliability, and willingness to do what was asked of him. I couldn't help but wonder if the lessons cemented in him by his Little League faithfulness might have helped him develop those characteristics. And yes, he actually got some playing time.

PERSEVERANCE

We all enjoy different skills, abilities, and gifts. Consequently, we will not all occupy the same station in life. Some of us will go on to great recognition, and others of us will labor quietly, in seeming obscurity, just like my dad. But we all can embrace perseverance and the stuff of consistent character development.

I love what Charles Haddon Spurgeon, the great British preacher, said: "It was by perseverance that the snail made it into the ark." That sentence triggers a scene in my mind of other animals passing the snail by. Most of them looked more elegant and prettier than the snail. Virtually all of them were more swift. But the snail eventually made it inside the ark anyway. Perseverance is really the foundation of anything that takes place in life. That's why I want to encourage those of you who are reading these words to never quit. Hang in there. Don't give up. Your perseverance, your model of tenacity even in the midst of opposition and painful choices in life, is providing the fuel for the next generation.

My dad frequently told us as we were growing up, "You know, I really want you all to go further and higher than I could ever go in my life. I'm working hard and I'm trying to do the very best that I can to provide you with what you need to go to the next level." Pop wasn't talking about public recognition. He was talking about character, godliness, impact, and making a difference with one's life in "going further and higher." In other words, Pop wanted us to show up, to be there with confidence, and to be reliable. His desire was that, no matter what, we would do all that was in our power to live in light of our commitment to what we said.

WAITING FOR DAD

Several years ago I heard a moving story about a family who lived in central Florida in a lovely home surrounded by a beautiful but very deep lake. They had two boys, an eleven-year-old son named Justin and a four-year-old son named Jason. One Saturday morning the wife and mother was out getting groceries. Dad and the two boys were out back working in the yard. Dad had to go inside the house to get something. Before he left, he reminded the two boys to stay close to the house and away from the dock because he knew that Jason could not swim. He assured the boys he wouldn't be gone long, but the phone rang as he went into the house. It was a friend, and the dad started what became a long conversation. Eventually he forgot about his sons being out in the back.

As might be expected, Justin and Jason became bored and began playing tag. As they played, their circle became bigger and bigger. They chased each other all over the yard and unfortunately their escapades finally took them out onto the dock. Jason, the four-year-old, was "it." As he tried to tag Justin on the dock, Justin sidestepped him and Jason fell into the water. Because it had rained, the water was murky. Justin couldn't see his brother in the water. He panicked and quickly ran into the house shouting, "Dad, Dad, Jason has fallen into the water!"

His father dropped the telephone, ran out onto the dock, dove into the water—and couldn't find his son. He came up for air, praying, "Oh, God, please help me find my boy." He went down again and something (or Someone) said to him, "Feel around the pilings of the dock." As he felt around the pilings, he felt the form of his son. Jason was holding onto the dock pilings. The father grabbed his boy and brought him to the surface. He stretched Jason out on the dock and performed CPR on him. To his amazement, the young fellow was fine after a few moments. As Jason came around, his father asked, "Son, can you tell me why you held onto the dock pilings when you went into the water?"

Jason responded, "Dad, I was waiting on you. I knew that you would show up."

That little four-year-old boy had already learned that he could count on his dad. He believed that his dad was a man of his word, a man of integrity. Jason just knew that if he hung in there long enough, Dad would be there.

Fellows, don't walk away. Show up. There are people all around us—some living under the same roof—who are holding onto the dock and waiting for us.

Questions and Application

1. What situations or categories of problems are most likely to contribute to your feeling like you want to give up? What can you do to face them successfully?

2. Do you have a trusted friend or small group to support you in prayer when you face difficult times? If so, meet with that friend or group in the next two weeks to talk over the first question. If not, try to find such a friend this week. (Hint: If you have problems finding a support group or friend, ask your pastor to help you connect with one.)

3. Do you know what difficulties face your wife and children this week? If not, ask them. Write them down and make it a point to pray today for their strength to face these challenges. Besides prayer, how else do you support your family members when they face situations that might tempt them to walk away from their responsibilities?

CHAPTER SIX

FOLLOW
THROUGH

"I speak one time."

Recently in our local grocery store I witnessed a scene that I had seen dozens of times before. I was waiting in the checkout line behind a mother and her little boy about four years old. He was full of energy—and completely out of control. He had his poor mother in an emotional upheaval. After a few minutes of watching this miniature Napoleon drive his mother to the threshold of insanity, it was obvious what was the problem: She was. Every time he would knock something over, touch something, or scream at her, she would say, "Billy, if you do that again, you're going to get it." But Billy never got it. She got it because Billy would do it again. He knew that dear, sweet Mom was full of threats but no action. Her empty warnings affirmed his chaotic behavior and totally eroded her authority.

Ephesians 6:1–4 says, "Children, obey your parents in the Lord, for this is right. Honor your father and mother (which is the first commandment with a promise), that it may be well with you, and that you may live long on the earth. And, fathers, do not provoke your children to anger; but bring them up in the discipline and instruction of the Lord."

I want to underscore verse 1: Paul says it is "right" for children to "obey." One of the most crucial mandates of parenting is to reinforce obedience and right choices in our children. Whenever a heart has not been cultivated to produce the fruit of obedience, then a life is overgrown with immoral weeds and self-centered, addictive behavior. As I walked out of that store, I thought, *Boy, does that mother need to tighten the reins on little Billy.* But my mind also flashed back to my childhood. As I opened my car door, I shook my head and said to no one in particular, "My sisters and I would have never been able to get away with that."

THE PATIENCE OF A MOTHER

Not to sound sexist in all of this, but I believe mothers tend to be more long-suffering with their children than fathers are. My mother was no exception. Mom has always been gentle and merciful. In fact, she's full of compassion and ever ready to smother a person with love. We could always count on Mom to go the extra mile and to give us that little ounce of grace and mercy that we needed when something wasn't done exactly when she wanted it done, or when we didn't follow through the first time. Mom was indeed long-suffering.

We knew that Mom had a flash point, but we also knew that it took her a while to reach it. So when she told us to do something, we knew she wasn't serious until she said it about the third time. (I know that she's probably reading these words now. Mom, don't get me for it *now.*) When we heard that certain growl in her voice, we knew it was time to put it in gear. Don't get me wrong. My mother was not afraid to mete out the consequences of disobedience. It's just that, given her personality, she was a little bit more tolerant and gave us more latitude.

You cannot be a successful parent and be afraid of your child.

Not so with Pop. When he clearly told me to do something and I didn't do it, he acted. Then, just in case I had forgotten his perspective on obedience, he would say, "I speak one time." We were not afraid of him. We knew he loved us and we knew that he would never abuse us, but there was something about his voice. It was a man's voice that communicated a little less tolerance than Mom's did in regard to our response when we had clearly heard and understood what he had said. It's not that he was mean and inflexible or that he ran our household as if he were some little demigod. In fact, he was not very demanding at all. We deeply respected both Pop and Mom. But we obeyed Pop quicker.

PEDOPHOBIA: FEAR OF ONE'S CHILDREN

Too many of us parents are afraid of our children. That might sound odd, but it's true. Karen and I speak in parenting conferences across the country. We're amazed at the number of questions we get related to discipline. A good many of those questions say more about the parents' problem than about the child's. Many times parents don't follow through with what they promise their children they will do simply because they are afraid the kids might reject them or not like them as much. So they resort to threats that they don't intend to carry out. Those threats really produce harmful results in the relationship. For one thing, such parents are not taken seriously by their children. You cannot be a successful parent and be afraid of your child.

Having said that, let me assure you that all of us succumb to the "not-following-through" syndrome from time to time. I can't think of one instance when I've disciplined our children for disobedience and enjoyed it. Nobody enjoys that; it's painful. Parents don't want to mete out consequences for disobedience, but it has to be done.

> *Our kids, just like us, rebel against God and against authority.*

When we were children, my father refused to get on our level and affirm our disobedience or procrastination by unnecessarily repeating himself. He felt it was a waste of time and energy to keep going over what had been discussed when we knew what had been said and we knew what the results of disobedience would be. Thus his admonition, "I speak one time."

This came up in our own household not long ago. My wife, Karen, was having a discussion with one of our children. I overheard it, and when they had finished talking, I simply asked her, "Honey, why are you having this unnecessary discussion with this child about something you plainly said to do? It is obvious that this child understood it, you understood it, and, for whatever reason, the child just didn't do it."

If my father told me to cut the grass before he got home because I wanted the privilege of using the car that weekend, and he came home and noticed the grass wasn't cut, he calmly said, "Son, I assume that you have made your decision not to use the car." If we knew the consequences of disobedience (or delayed obedience) and did not do what he said, Pop simply figured that we preferred the consequences. Pop did whatever he could to meet all of our needs, but he was also a man with a deep set of convictions, and one of them had to do with obedience and respect. In this regard, if we forced him, he felt it was more important to be respected than it was to be liked.

THE MYTH OF THE ALWAYS ADORED PARENT

Let's face it: Through the course of our children's lives as they grow up in our homes, there are many times when they won't like us as parents. We have to say or do things that run against their grain. In response to our discipline, children will often have crying spells or pouting spells, be non-communicative, or even walk away to demonstrate that they don't like us very much at the moment. They may even say, "I don't love you." These are weapons of control that can be effective against unsuspecting parents, but there are some things about which we must hold our ground in spite of their reactions. We must stand firm about certain principles related to obedience and respect. I realize that, given the current environment in some Christian circles, what I'm saying may not be particularly palatable.

People are writing articles and books about how to have kids like you and obey you at the same time. Well, the truth is, our children have sin natures. Our kids, just like us, rebel against God and against authority. There are times that they won't do what we ask them to do or what is right. At that point, we have to realize that it is more important for us to embrace truth than it is to meet them on their territory and on their level. But pointing out sin for what it is won't always help us win a popularity contest with our children.

> *Respecting authority . . .*
> *is really the core issue when it*
> *comes to obedience and consequences.*

Please don't misunderstand me. I think we have to choose our battles as parents, and not every issue is worth "going to the mat" for. But when it has to do with basic responsibilities of life, the Word of God, what is objectively true and right, or even the real rules of the household, then I think we have to draw some clear lines. You have to trust God to give you the courage and the strength to face up to your children and to let them know that there is order in the household. You must affirm that you are the parent and they are the children. Children should not lead parents. God has placed you in your children's lives to give direction and order, to bring them to a place where they can understand the gospel, to let them know what the parameters of life are all about, to help them understand the moral "time of day," and to provide them with what it takes to be a gift to the world rather than a curse to society.

HELPING YOUR KIDS GROW INTO RESPONSIBILITY

Certainly as a child gets older there needs to be a reduction in the number of demands that we make on them. Hopefully at critical points in their development—as they move toward adolescence, as they get a little bit older, after they leave home—they prove themselves to be progressively more responsible for their own choices and actions. However, the foundation for respecting authority should have been firmly laid by then. That is really the core issue when it comes to obedience and consequences.

I believe that the first six or seven years are the most critical years in a child's development when it comes to his relationship to authority. It's in those early years that we as parents make our word reliable or not. That determines whether we are taken seriously or not. Throughout those years, our children are formulating their perspectives on authority, and those perspectives depend to a large degree on our ability to make good on our promises.

It is important to understand that at this stage in a child's development, authority is eroded by needless explanations. When I went off to college, I "learned" that my father was wrong. I learned in some introductory courses to psychology and other family-related subjects that one should never tell a child "Because I said so" when he asks for an explanation. The reason "the experts" gave for this was that such a response stifles children's development and creativity; it hinders them from taking the initiative in their lives and from understanding reasoning. The thinking was, the sooner children can understand reasoning and apply it to their lives, the more they will develop self-determination. Well, now that I have four children and have become a little bit more astute in the games that kids can play, I'm glad to say that I have returned to my father's perspective. Understand, Pop allowed us to ask questions. He didn't just always bottom-line things.

I think we *ought* to engage our children and let them know on a regular basis the reasons that we have to discipline them or the reasons we do certain things. However, a five- or six-year-old child does not always need to have a reason for what you have said or what you have told him to do. It is highly appropriate at times simply to say "Because I said so," and that should be good enough. It's true that we don't want our kids growing up to be led astray by anybody in a position of authority, but still, we do want them to appreciate authority. It's another fact of life: We all live under authority, and sometimes an explanation is not needed.

---

*Tangible consequences
produce tangible results.*

Whenever you give in to the mind games and the power plays of your children, you set them up for a miserable life. Bratty, whiny kids who never had a wholesome respect for authority "grow up" (using the term loosely here) to be bratty, whiny adults who are self-centered and often have difficulty maintaining relationships or being productive at all. Again, respect for authority is a very serious issue.

BEING TAKEN SERIOUSLY BY YOUR KIDS

I learned five things from my father when it comes to this whole issue of being taken seriously when you speak. The first one is *don't waste words.* Don't add a lot of apologies or unnecessary detail that make you look timid. Secondly, *don't threaten.* What good does a threat do to anybody? Thirdly, *be clear about expectations.* When you tell someone, especially a child, how to behave or what to do, make sure you both are very clear about what you expect. Number four, *be clear about consequences,* particularly if your expectations involve an area with which that child has struggled in the past. Finally, if need be, *take clear, decisive action.*

Around our house, our children have chores and responsibilities. Whether it's taking out the trash, cutting the grass, cleaning the kitchen, or simply cleaning their rooms, everyday life at home reminds them that they have responsibilities. Our house is just like many other houses, though; often there would be squabbles and arguments about who was supposed to do what. Then Karen and I would have to get in there and try to figure out why certain things hadn't been done. Needless to say, we'd hear a lot of excuses.

A few years ago, my wife came up with a great idea that minimized the lack of follow-through on job responsibilities around the house. At that time our children all received allowances. We'd put their allowances in various envelopes. Each child had three envelopes: One was for giving to the Lord, one was for savings, and the third was for entertainment and recreation. In our new system, every time there was a job for which a child was responsible and that job was not done, we'd go and collect a dollar from his or her allowance. They weren't getting a whole lot of money. In fact, before they figured out the system there were several instances when they went into the hole financially. We were amazed at how the arguments and excuses subsided in a matter of weeks. Since our children are capitalists, that set of consequences really worked.

Tangible consequences produce tangible results. Say what you mean and back up your words with action. It's a testimony to your integrity and an example your children will carry with them throughout their lives.

Questions and Application

1. Have you programmed your children to hear you repeat yourself several times before they have to take action?

What can you learn from the Loritts family examples in this chapter to make your consequences firm, but not exercised from anger?

2. If you know you have to speak more than once for your children to respond obediently, set aside some time in the next few days for a quick family meeting to discuss how things will change as you "speak once." Don't forget to clearly list consequences for inaction, but also remember that you may need to stage in those consequences. After all, your children didn't learn the pattern overnight, but over time. The process of "unlearning" will take time, too.

PART THREE

OUT OF
DISCIPLINE
COMES INTEGRITY

CHAPTER SEVEN

ACKNOWLEDGE SHAME

"You hurt my heart."

One of the most important days in my life was in 1962. It came after the only time I ever stole anything—and I was caught. It was a warm spring day in Newark, and I was walking to school with a few of my friends. We were all about twelve years old; I was particularly vulnerable to peer pressure at that time. On our way to school, we passed a factory that made chains for various kinds of necklaces. A few open boxes of their wares sat on the sidewalk. Several of my friends threw out the idea that we ought to take some of those chains; after all, they were right there in front of us. Overcome by mutual peer pressure and temptation, we decided to scoop up a few handfuls and run like crazy.

The story doesn't end there. Over the next few weeks, these same friends of mine decided to steal several boxes of chains. They were caught. Worse, they said that I was part of their group, even though I had not been with them on other occasions when they had stolen.

A PAINFUL LESSON

I will never forget the evening the police came to our apartment. My father worked nights, but he happened to be off that evening. (As I look back on it now, this was a divine appointment for a life-changing lesson.) When confronted with the charges in the presence of my father, I decided to do what every normal, sinful twelve-year-old boy would do: I lied. But Pop made me open my dresser drawers and, to my horror, beneath my undershorts were those chains.

A contrite heart . . . remembers the pain that the sin has caused.

I thought my life had come to an end. The officer said that the manager of the factory wanted to see my friends and me. My other three friends were down in the patrol car. Pop asked the officer if he could take the boys out of the patrol car and drive them down to the factory. (He couldn't stand the sight of three preteens in a police car.) So my father drove us to the factory. He drove in deafening silence. When we arrived at the factory, he made us own up to what we did, apologize, and offer to pay for what we had stolen. The manager graciously said that he did not want to press charges, but he wanted to make sure we had learned our lesson. Pop drove the other three boys home and made me stand next to him as he explained to their mothers (none of them had fathers in the home) what had happened at the factory.

When we got home, he told me that he was going to spank me, and then he gave me a long list of things that I would not be able to do for quite a while. Then he did something that tore my heart out; it was far worse than any spanking. Pop cried. Up until that point I had only seen my father cry twice, and that was at the funerals of his brother and his sister. He said to me, "Boy, if you wanted something, why didn't you ask me? You don't ever have to steal anything." Then came the clincher. Pop said, "You hurt my heart." I had brought shame to him and violated his trust in me. That evening a twelve-year-old boy made up his mind that he would never hurt his dad like that again. Whenever I was tempted to take something that did not belong to me, I saw that tear trickling down my father's cheek.

BROKENNESS AND CONTRITION

Most scholars believe that David wrote Psalm 51 expressing his sorrow, shame, and deep repentance concerning the adultery he had committed with Bathsheba. Feel the deep agony and remorse of David's heart as you read these words. Look especially at verses 10–12: "Create in me a clean heart, O God, and renew a steadfast spirit within me. Do not cast me away from Thy presence, and do not take Thy Holy Spirit from me. Restore to me the joy of Thy salvation, and sustain me with a willing spirit." Then consider verses 16 and 17: "For Thou dost not delight in sacrifice, otherwise I would give it; Thou art not pleased with burnt offering. The sacrifices of God are a broken spirit; a broken and a contrite heart, O God, Thou wilt not despise."

I want you to notice those two words in verse 17—"broken" and "contrite." To be broken has to do with understanding that I have come to the end of myself; that in my human nature, I don't have the resources to please God. On the surface that sounds very negative, but it's actually a positive thing. Brokenness expresses my need for, and total reliance upon, someone greater than myself. When I'm broken,

I realize that I must completely trust in God's sufficiency. *Brokenness* in this context has to do with David coming to the end of himself with regard to his sin. *Contrition* has to do with the permanent sorrow of remembering the pain that his sin caused.

I think sometimes we confuse guilt with contrition. We know as Christians that the moment we confess our sins, they're taken care of. That's what 1 John 1:9 says: "If we confess our sins, He is faithful and righteous to forgive us our sins and to cleanse us from all unrighteousness." Certainly, we should not feel guilty about our forgiven sin. But I think it's a tragic error to ask God to erase the *pain* that our sin caused, and that's what contrition is: remembering the pain that our sin caused. In Psalm 51:17, David wrote that the sacrifices of God are a broken spirit and a contrite heart. That heart remembers the pain that the sin has caused.

I have a callus on the bottom of my right foot. A number of years ago, I stepped on a huge twenty-penny nail that went through my sneaker and almost clear through my foot. As the doctor examined my foot, he told me that it would heal with no problem. However, he added that because of the wound's location, I would have trouble with a callus there for the rest of my life. As the doctor promised, there's no problem with the wound, but every once in a while when I step on my foot the wrong way, there's a painful little reminder of what took place more than two decades ago. So it is with sin in our lives, and this is the goal of contrition: The act of remembering the pain that our sin caused in the past serves as a deterrent to committing or repeating further sin.

HOLDING CHILDREN
ACCOUNTABLE FOR THEIR SINS

Every cute, cuddly, warm child who brings so much joy to our hearts at birth is a sinner—and children *will* sin. Karen and I made up our minds a long time ago that we would not make excuses for the sins of our children, nor would we hide our hurt and disappointment when they sin. This may sound cruel to some people, but it is good to let your children know when they've disappointed you with their behavior. Bryndan said to us recently, "When you let me know that I've done something wrong, it makes me want to make things right—and to make them right as soon as possible."

I firmly believe that we are guilty of spiritual and moral child abuse whenever we legitimize our children's immoral, dishonest, or disrespectful behavior by either ignoring it or somehow minimizing its impact. To engage in this kind of immediate "damage control" only guarantees future character disintegration. It is our obligation to let our children know when they have hurt our hearts and, most importantly, the heart of God by their actions.

> *We cannot even know God*
> *without first knowing shame.*

There's an old-fashioned word that has become tainted and tarnished by our morally drifting culture, and that's the word "shame." We don't want to take responsibility for our own behavior and choices in life. It is easier to blame my immoral, bad behavior on other people, my background, my tendencies toward codependency, or how I was rejected sometime. It's easy to deflect my personal responsibility to somebody else's faults or failures.

To be sure, we all carry emotional scars. Emotional pain

contributes to all kinds of bad behavior, but we are living in a society in which we don't want to own any sense of responsibility when we have done wrong. In fact, we reject any objective truth about what is right and what is wrong. Tragically, even many of our Bible-believing evangelical circles have adopted this kind of moral cloudiness. We want to affirm one another.

Under the banner of "being sensitive," we don't want to come across as being legalistic or projecting guilt trips on other people. The result? We don't encourage taking personal responsibility for our choices. We think that feeling bad about what one has done is equal to having low self-esteem, which is a culturally unacceptable thing to have. We believe it's a greater sin for us to push people toward feelings of guilt and remorse than it is for them to continue in sin. Christians can even justify their failure to hold each other accountable with the line, "Really, that's what the Holy Spirit does in people's lives. It's not my job to judge people." But shame and sorrow are good things. We *ought* to feel bad about doing bad. We *should* be ashamed of some things. Even *Webster's Third New International Dictionary* defines "shame" as "a painful emotion caused by consciousness of guilt, shortcoming or impropriety of one's own behavior or position, or in the behavior of a closely associated person or group."

When the former chairman of the Joint Chiefs of Staff, General Colin Powell, addressed the 1996 Republican Convention, he said that we need to restore a sense of shame in our culture to reinforce right behavior choices. Amen. I cheered at that. Some things are objectively right and some are objectively wrong. Shame can be a deterrent to making wrong choices. It can be a powerful, God-given handicap that keeps us dependent upon Him for the strength and courage to overcome our weaknesses. If we don't acknowledge that we have anything to overcome, or if we are constantly blaming other people for our problems, then we can't grow and we can't overcome our weaknesses.

We cannot even know God without first knowing shame. Shame is God's way of convincing us in the deep recesses of our being that we desperately need forgiveness. Shame drives us to the point of seeking that forgiveness and of being willing to make any change necessary in order to secure it. There is no such thing as lasting character development apart from acknowledging shame. Shame is part of the conviction of the Holy Spirit, and it is the prerequisite for change.

In the providence of God,
Pop let me see his pain and his hurt.

In John 16:8, Jesus described the work of the Holy Spirit this way: "And He, when He comes, will convict the world concerning sin, and righteousness, and judgment." Conviction should always lead to repentance. The word "convict" simply means "convinced that we are wrong." Repentance is the proper human response to our wrongdoing. When we repent, there has to be a change of direction; accompanying that change of direction is a heart that is ashamed and sorrowful. In 2 Corinthians 7, the apostle Paul wrote about the productive nature of sorrow and shame. He said in verses 9 and 10, "I now rejoice, not that you were made sorrowful, but that you were made sorrowful to the point of repentance; for you were made sorrowful according to the will of God, in order that you might not suffer loss in anything through us. For the sorrow that is according to the will of God produces a repentance without regret, leading to salvation; but the sorrow of the world produces death."

My father's response to my sinful behavior on that spring day in 1962 drove me to understand shame. I shudder to think where I might be today if my father had winked at the situation and said, "That's just a childhood prank; boys will be boys." With such a response, Pop might have initiated a lifestyle of behavior in me that would have landed me in prison someplace. In the providence of God, Pop let me see his pain and his hurt. In so doing, not only did he counteract my wrong behavior by allowing me to pay consequences, but he also showed me his heart because of the depth of his love for me.

BEING RESPONSIBLE FOR ONE'S OWN SINS

Shame and sorrow ought to work both ways. There have been any number of times (I can't count them all) in which Karen and I have had to go back to our children and apologize to them for things we have done that have hurt or disappointed them. We have learned that we need to model the courage to repent and to admit our own shame before our children.

Recently I got a fresh reminder of this. At this writing, we're teaching Bryndan how to drive. (What an experience!) Bryndan prefers driving his mother's car because it's smaller than mine and easier for him to maneuver, but I feel very strongly that he needs to know how to drive my car so that while he's learning he can become acquainted with various sizes. Because he's anxious to drive, it usually doesn't take much coaxing from me to have Bryndan drive my car while I'm in it. However, one morning Bryndan protested when I asked him to drive my car on the trip to take Holly and him to school. He just didn't want to drive my car. I was tired and under a lot of stress from ministry that morning, so I pushed him: "Son, *drive this car.* I'm not asking you, I'm *telling* you." Bryndan was very upset. He went ahead and drove the car while I said some really direct things to him about his attitude.

After I'd let the kids off and started on the way to my office, I became convicted. *I don't know why I acted that way,* I thought while my heart sank. *What was the big deal? Bryndan's a great kid, and if he didn't want to drive the car, he didn't really need to drive the car. Why are you pushing him, Crawford?* I felt awful about it, and I knew what I had to do. Before I made it to the office, I turned around and went back to Bryndan's school.

I went to the attendance office and asked if I could see my son. They paged him and he came to the office. When he saw me, I said to him, "Bryndan, that was terrible. I'm sorry. I shouldn't have pushed you. If you didn't want to drive the car, you didn't have to drive the car. I blew it, Son. Would you please forgive me?"

Bryndan smiled, hugged me, and said, "Dad, you came all the way back here just to tell me that? That's no big deal." We hugged right there in the attendance office. Bryndan said, "Look, man, have a good day." He went off to class, I went to my office, and we *both* had good days.

As with most men, apologies don't come easy for me. Yet I've learned through the passage of time that the way to draw someone closer to you is to acknowledge your own need and to admit when you are wrong. It reinforces the fact that you're accessible to that person. My kids feel more comfortable in acknowledging their own wrong and admitting their own shame when they see repentance modeled by Karen and me.

It's a shame that shame doesn't get the credit for the good it can do.

Questions and Application

1. Can you think of an example from your own childhood when admitting shame helped you? Can you tell that story in such a way that it could help your children? Try it.

2. Take a few moments to talk with your spouse about how you let your children know when they've disappointed you. Are there ways to improve that process? What are they? How do you follow through to help your children make positive changes as a result of those encounters?

CHAPTER EIGHT

CALL FOR RESPECT

"They have theirs; you need to get yours."

A few months ago I was preaching in a town just a few miles away from Newark, where I was born and raised. I flew in on Saturday, and since I wasn't scheduled to do anything that Saturday evening, I decided to drive down to the old neighborhood where I'd spent the first twelve years of my life. Mind you, I had not been back in many, many years; I didn't really know what to expect. In fact, I sort of surprised myself when I was able to feel my way through the streets of Newark and pick up some familiar road markers to find the old neighborhood.

When I got there I was really surprised. In fact, my heart was a little disappointed. I had a picture of what it used to be like that was sort of a freeze-frame in my mind. When I saw how different things are now, I was grateful for the progress but also sad because there was very little there that reminded me of the way things used to be. *This used to be the Loritts family's neighborhood,* I thought. But instead of seeing the familiar old apartment buildings and houses, I saw all new structures. Our old apartment building had been torn down, and there were townhouses all over the place to show evidence of a resurgence of the community.

> *Pop never cared much*
> *for the popular truism*
> *that "respect is earned."*

Yet there were two things that I was surprised were still intact. One was the church we used to attend, Trinity AME Zion Church on the corner of Wilsey and Warren. The other was my elementary school. Remarkably, it looked exactly the way it looked in the 1950s when I walked through those halls. I easily recognized the playground where I played softball and dodgeball with my buddies. As I slowly drove around the school, I looked up at the classroom windows and remembered the teachers, the sounds, the laughter, and all of the great times during those years I attended Warren Street Elementary School.

PAYING ONE'S DUES

My mind was flooded with a deluge of memories. I remembered coming home from school, doing homework, field trips, and all of those things. But I also remembered something Pop said to my sisters and me whenever we complained about how hard or unfair we felt a teacher was. He'd sort of smile at us and say, "Well, they have theirs; you need to get yours." This was Pop's way of stressing the importance of paying our dues. He felt that if we were going to criticize someone, especially someone in a position of authority, then we needed to do it carefully and realize that the person had walked the path before us. Respect and honor were the issues with Pop. If a person was older or in a position of authority, then we respected that person, no questions asked. Pop never cared much for the popular truism that "respect is earned." He believed that if people did not live as if they respected themselves, then you still respected their position, their age, or the simple fact that they were human beings.

This perspective is deeply rooted in the Scriptures. The Bible is replete with injunctions, admonishments, and illustrations of the importance of giving respect. Let me point your attention to one passage, 1 Peter 2:13–17:

> Submit yourselves for the Lord's sake to every human institution, whether to a king as the one in authority, or to governors as sent by him for the punishment of evildoers and the praise of those who do right. For such is the will of God that by doing right you may silence the ignorance of foolish men. Act as free men, and do not use your freedom as a covering for evil, but use it as bondslaves of God. Honor all men; love the brotherhood, fear God, honor the king.

The emphasis in this text is on our attitude and behavior, not necessarily on whether those people in positions of authority "deserve" our respect. Peter was more concerned about Christians doing what was right than whether or not somebody else did what was right.

A RESPECTFUL NAME

My father took this injunction to heart. For example, we were never allowed to call older people by their first names or to become too casual or familiar with them. When we got out of line, he would quickly and clearly remind us that we were speaking to an adult and not to one of our playmates. We had to call people by "Mr." or "Miss" or "Mrs." or "Reverend" or "Doctor" or whatever the person's official title was, as long as it reflected a sense of respect. Even with those who were close to our family, we never used their first name alone. We had to call them "Uncle Robert" or "Aunt Hattie."

That was so ingrained in me that even to this day I have a hard time calling anyone who is much older than me by his first name. I'll never forget an incident with Dr. Bill Bright, the founder and president of Campus Crusade for Christ—and my boss. A number of years ago, when I first joined Campus Crusade's staff, I persisted in calling him "Dr. Bright" in private meetings. Finally, one day, he reached over and said, "Crawford, you can call me Bill."

The respect issue needs to be a core value in our homes.

Whenever our children call older people by their first names, I'll say, "Put a handle on that." They know what I mean: Call the person "Mr." or "Coach" or "Uncle" or "Auntie" or something, but don't just use a first name. Increasingly, the concept of respect means very little in our culture. We're very casual about people in positions of authority. We feel as if we have every right to be demeaning and to poke fun at anyone, even the president of the United States (if he's from another party). Elderly people are not given much honor and dignity, and I think part of it is because of the way we allow our children to exercise a casual mind-set about people—even people who are in positions of responsibility in society. That needs to be corrected as they are growing up. We need to help them embrace the concept of respect. I'm not talking about blind allegiance or blind loyalty; I'm not talking about endorsing terrible behavior. To respect someone does not mean that we agree with the person, but it means that we honor people for either their position or the fact that they are human beings.

By example, Pop demonstrated that the core of respect is the realization that you cannot control what someone else does or how another person lives, but you can control your response to him and treat him with dignity. However, he also stressed that we had to carry ourselves in such a way as to make it easy for people to respect us. We couldn't control the responses of others, but we needed to control our own behavior to make sure that there weren't barriers people had to overcome in order to respect us.

RESPECTING POP'S PARTNER

Mom had to handle "extra duty" during the week because Pop worked at night. Pop had to be at work by four in the afternoon and didn't make it home until well after midnight. Some weeks we wouldn't even see Pop except for the weekend and the one day a week he had off. On the days Pop worked, we'd be in school when he left for work and in bed by the time he made it home.

I'm convinced that the love and respect that my sisters and I have for Pop are not only due to his love and commitment to his family, but are also due in a large part to Mom's commitment to Pop and to the unity of her family. To this day, my mother is a living, breathing example of sacrificial love and teamwork. She kept the needs of her husband and family above her own.

We witnessed Mom's love for us every day. She awoke early every morning to fix us breakfast. She saw to it that her children were clean, well dressed, and ready for school. Mom was the first person we saw when we burst through the apartment door after school. She was there to fix our physical and emotional bruises. Although Mom is a sweet and gentle person, she was no wimp when it came to discipline. When Pop wasn't home, she took over that responsibility without reluctance.

Mom said no to anything that would directly compete for her attention to her family. After we children came along, Mom waited until I was in the fourth grade to take a job outside the home. Mom and Pop deferred their dream of owning a house until they felt we children were old enough to deal with both of them working. Then they began their effort to work and save money for a house in earnest. Even then, Mom's job was within walking distance of our apartment so she would be home within the hour when we came home from school.

The first thing Mom said when she came home from work in those years was, "Tell me about your day." She expected a report with a few details that would show that we'd actually learned something at school. Then she made dinner for us and helped us with our homework. If we had a late afternoon or evening activity, Mom made sure we were there on time—and more often than not, she was there with us. (Believe me, by the time Mom started working it seemed my sisters and I *always* had places to go and things to do.)

For some years after I became a parent myself, I wondered where Mom found the energy to do all she did. Once the answer came to me, I was almost embarrassed because it should have been obvious: Mom prayed. My mother is a woman of God. I can't tell you the number of times growing up that I walked past my parents' bedroom and saw my mother on her knees crying out to God on behalf of her family. God has been, and continues to be, the source of her life and strength. She knew *she* didn't have the strength on her own to raise a family. She knew that she and Pop alone couldn't do a complete job of it, either. But Mom knew that God had everything that she needed, and she was never afraid to go to Him for an abundant supply.

Mom always presented Pop to us in the best light possible. Because he worked at night there were times, try as he might, that Pop had to miss a game or an event that was important to us. Sometimes I'd complain to Mom, "I wish Pop were here."

She'd always tell me, "You know your daddy would break his neck to be here with you if he could. But he has to work so we can have a roof over our heads, clothes on our backs, and food in our stomachs." Then Mom would recount a list of things Pop *had* done with us recently.

Mom had an astounding gift for putting things in perspective. In so many ways, Mom was the cement that kept the Loritts household together. That's why Pop loved her so much. That's why he demanded that we respect her.

I remember a time when I was fifteen that I disagreed with Mom about something (for the life of me, I can't remember what) and raised my voice to her.

That was all it took for Pop. He intervened that instant. He placed his hand on my shoulder, made sure I was looking him in the eye, and said calmly, "Son, she was my wife before she was your mother. You will never talk to her that way again in this house. Go ask her to forgive you—*now.*"

I did. I never forgot Pop's admonition that day. I'm glad I didn't, because I had the chance to use it myself years later.

Every child will test the limits. One time Bryndan was "kissing the line" with a disrespectful response to his mother. He didn't realize that I was in the adjoining room. When he made those comments to Karen, I came around the corner and he saw me. I thought the boy was going to die of a heart attack, because he knew not only that he had gone over the line, but also that I was not as merciful as his mother in situations like that. I simply said to him, "Son, you will never talk to my wife that way again. She was my wife before she was your mother." I purposely put it that way for him to know that there is a strong boundary that he would not trespass. He understood that disrespect toward his mother would not be tolerated.

I think Bryndan will remember my admonition to him. Maybe his children will be the generation that won't require hearing it!

THE CORE VALUE OF RESPECT

I believe very strongly that the respect issue needs to be a core value in our homes. Whenever our children come in contact with authority figures, we need to reinforce the concept of respect and make sure that they are embracing it. First of all, respect begins in the home. Let me strongly suggest that you never let a child get away with disrespectful attitudes or words in your presence. Your child should never be allowed to talk back to you as the parent. You should never engage in a dialogue of talking back and shouting to one another. That's a formula for chaos. To do that means to leave your position of authority and to get down to his level, which means that you have essentially lost the battle. Children, being who they are, will always test the boundaries and the limits. When they do, adults need to stand firm.

Sometimes when our kids get around other people (particularly in school), they get a case of amnesia concerning the values and principles they've learned at home. It's at those junctures that we have to go back and underscore the lessons.

Holly, our younger daughter, recently called home, and I was there to answer the phone. "Dad, I missed the school bus," she began.

"Why did you miss the school bus?"

"I had an activity and I was running late. The assistant principal wouldn't let me go out of the door that was nearest the bus. By the time I got around there I'd missed the bus."

As I went to pick her up, I saw the assistant principal and said, "Holly says that you wouldn't let her go through that side door." Then he told me the complete story. It was true that he wouldn't let her go through the side door, but it was also true that my daughter had been very disrespectful to him.

When I found Holly, I asked, "Honey, is what the assistant principal told me true?" She acknowledged sadly that it was, and tears filled her eyes. Holly is probably our most tender and merciful child. I made her go to him and, while I was standing there, look him in the eye and ask his forgiveness for being disrespectful.

On another occasion, during Bryan's senior year of high school, I had to run by the house in the middle of the afternoon. While I was there the phone rang. I picked up the telephone and heard the voice of one of Bryan's teachers. The teacher asked, "Is Bryan there?"

I answered, "No, he's supposed to be in school."

"I had to ask your son to leave the classroom because he was being disrespectful."

I was shocked. "You mean Bryan Loritts, our son? You asked him to leave because he was being disrespectful?"

Bryan had never been in any trouble at all at school, but his teacher replied, "Yes, and we don't know where he is."

"I'll be right there." I hopped in my car and hurried over to Bryan's school. Sure enough, Bryan was not at the attendance office where he was supposed to be. I went down to the gym. There he was, shooting baskets when he was supposed to be in the attendance office.

"Son, what in the world is going on here? Why did you get kicked out of class?"

Respect reflects a heart for the dignity of all humanity.

Evidently there had been a misunderstanding. Bryan jokingly called another kid a name he should not have called him, and the teacher thought the name was directed at him. The teacher demanded he leave and go to the attendance office, and at that point Bryan mouthed off to him and told him he wasn't going. He simply disregarded the teacher and went to the gym. I had my son come with me to stand and look the teacher squarely in the eye.

"Son, you've got something to say to this man, don't you?"

Bryan said to his teacher, "No matter how I disagree with you, sir, I'm sorry. What I did was wrong. I was disrespectful and I should not have done that."

We did some other things to guarantee that that would not happen again. As adults, we too sometimes forget the importance of respect. But respect is a very important issue.

Not long ago, my younger son and I were in downtown Atlanta to shop. As we were walking down the street, we saw a homeless man lying on the street. He was filthy and unkempt, and to add insult to his injury he had just urinated all over himself. He looked pitiful. Bryndan and I saw this and I said to my son, "Bryndan, I want you to look at that man. I never want you to forget, Son, that that man is somebody's son. That man could be somebody's father. That man could be somebody's brother. But, more important, that man is a human being who has been created in the image of God. And I never want you to forget, Son, that there but for the grace of God goes you. You could be just like that man. And that man deserves some love, dignity, and respect."

Respect not only acknowledges the importance of authority and order in culture and society, but it also has everything to do with compassion. Respect reflects a heart for the dignity of all humanity, no matter where it may be found.

God grant that it may be found in generous measure in our homes.

Questions and Application

1. What makes it difficult for you to respect some people? Do you see those same difficulties reflected in your children? What's the best way you can think of to explain to your kids why respect is so important? Tell them that explanation this week.

2. How do you help your children respect your spouse? Their teachers? Your pastor?

3. What are some ways you show your children respect?

CHAPTER NINE

PROTECT
YOUR FAMILY

"You will never put your hands on him again."

Driving through the old neighborhood in Newark that Saturday evening and wandering past the Warren Street Elementary School triggered another memory —an incident in which I saw a side of Pop that I'd never seen before.

As I recall, it was pretty early in the afternoon of a very warm day in the summer of 1960. Since he worked nights, my father was home during the day. The school playground ran summer programs, complete with a recreation director to oversee all of the kids' activities. I was involved in a game of softball when a truck came through the playground to carry away the residue from cleaning out the old coal furnace in the bottom of the school. When the truck came by, the softball rolled behind the truck. In the past, some of the kids had jumped on the back of the truck to "catch a ride." When I went to recover the ball, the recreation director, a man in his late twenties or early thirties, looked up and assumed that I was trying to catch a ride on the back of the truck. He began yelling at me. Before I knew it, he was telling me to leave the playground.

I protested. I tried to explain to him that I hadn't been trying to get on the back of the truck. At that point he started toward me. Rather than allowing me to walk away from the playground on my own, he grabbed me, twisted my arm into a hammerlock behind me, and literally pushed me down the steps from the playground. I suppose there were ten or twelve concrete steps that he pushed me down. I remember the embarrassment because the incident took place in front of my friends. Through tears I told him, "I'm going to go home and tell my father." I guess he thought that was an empty threat. I ran home; we lived only a couple of blocks from the playground.

I was crying frantically when I ran into the building, up the three flights of steps to our apartment, and through the door. Pop saw me and said, "Boy, what in the world is wrong with you?" Then I told him the story of the recreation director twisting my arm and pushing me down the steps.

I am putting an exclamation mark to one of the primary roles of a husband and a father: to do whatever it takes to protect his family.

Pop was livid. I'll never forget his face. He stood to his feet and he said, "Now, boy, I want to make sure you are telling me the truth. You didn't do anything. Now he actually touched you and pushed you down the steps?" I explained it all to him again. Pop nodded and said, "You come with me." He grabbed me by the hand and we went down to the playground.

As we walked onto the playground, my father stopped to ask a couple of my friends their version of the incident. They told him the same story that I had told him. Then, with me in tow, he briskly walked right to the recreation director. He stood toe-to-toe with him and asked, "Now, sir, did you put your hands on my son?"

The man became very indignant with my dad. He answered, "Yes, I did," almost as if to say "And what are *you* going to do about it?"

Well, that was the wrong answer. I never knew Pop to be violent, but he was a very strong man. He grabbed the man by his shirt with both hands and literally lifted him off his feet, slammed him up against the fence, and said, "You will never put your hands on him again." I was petrified. I had never seen that side of my father. I'd never seen him hit or touch anybody. I suppose my eyes were as big as saucers; my heart was racing. I actually thought my father was going to punch the man's lights out.

THE ROLE OF PROTECTOR

In today's world, I think my father probably would have handled that situation a little differently. But what impressed me was my dad's incredible commitment to me, his son, in that he would do whatever it took to protect me. Pop was not violent, although he was tough; in this particular setting he believed it was necessary to show his strength to get the man's attention and protect me.

Let me note here that respect had been so ingrained in me by my father that I didn't think for a minute that his strong response to the man gave me an excuse to show disrespect to the recreation director in the future. With today's generation of children, respect is a tougher battle; fathers doing such a thing today would not only risk danger to their own lives, but they would probably find their kids cheering the reaction and responding to the man with a smug "You got yours; don't mess with me again" attitude.

Violence is distasteful, and it's terrible. I'm not promoting violence at all, but I am putting an exclamation mark to one of the primary roles of a husband and a father: to do whatever it takes to protect his family. I believe this is at the heart of what Peter was saying in 1 Peter 5:1–3. Admittedly, the passage has to do with spiritual leaders within the context of the church, but I think a good secondary application has to do with the role of a father in the home. Peter wrote,

> Therefore, I exhort the elders among you, as your fellow elder and witness of the sufferings of Christ, and a partaker also of the glory that is to be revealed, shepherd the flock of God among you, exercising oversight not under compulsion, but voluntarily, according to the will of God; and not for sordid gain, but with eagerness; nor yet as lording it over those allotted to your charge, but proving to be examples to the flock.

My dad was a shepherd of his flock at home. We all knew that wherever he was, there was safety. Leadership in the home has both to do with *direction* and *protection*. It not only has to do with pointing our children toward the direction they should go, but it also has to do with creating the environment in which they can have a relative degree of safety.

THE PRINCIPLE OF PROTECTION

Pop's response to that recreation director burned in my heart that this is part of what a man does for his wife and children. At the center of my father's response was the fact that he didn't abuse his children, so he wasn't going to let anybody else do it either. Again, let me say that I'm not talking about people taking the law into their own hands and returning violence for violence. The principle of protection goes beyond "duking it out" with a recreation director. It is making sure that we are securing a safe environment in which our children can grow and develop without being taken advantage of, either physically or emotionally.

Bryndan's Bully

My children know that I will do all that is within me to protect them simply because in the summer of 1960 I saw that my father would not allow certain things to happen to his boy. I've had any number of opportunities to provide protection for our children. I remember a few years back when our younger son was about twelve years old. A neighborhood bully was considerably older than Bryndan, probably around eighteen years old. I was out of town, unfortunately, when this incident took place.

Bryndan was playing basketball with a group at a friend's house. The kids there were all about Bryndan's age and Joey (that's not his real name), this eighteen-year-old bully, came by, took the basketball from Bryndan, and then shoved him and punched him in his chest for good measure. Bryndan came home and told his mother and a very good friend of our family. Karen and our friend took immediate care of the situation; they went and talked to this young man and sort of straightened things out. Bryndan wasn't really hurt, but it was bothersome that this older fellow was terrorizing my son and was really nothing more than a "wannabe" hoodlum.

The next day I arrived home and was briefed on what had taken place. It just so happened that I had to go run an errand. As I was driving down the street, I saw Joey walking up the street. I stopped the car and motioned for Joey to come over. He did. I calmly but directly said to him, "Young man, I heard what happened yesterday. I just want you to know that this will never happen again. As Bryndan's father, I will do everything within my power to make *sure* that it won't happen again." I then proceeded to share a few other perspectives with him. The bottom line is that, since then, Joey has never even come close to doing anything unkind to Bryndan.

Children Protecting Each Other

It's amazing to see the natural tendency to protect my family come out in our children, especially our two boys. During Bryan's freshman year in college he came home on a vacation. I noticed one evening around the dinner table that Bryan was unusually quiet. I asked, "Son, what seems to be the problem?"

Bryan replied, "Well, Dad, today I went over to the high school to visit some of my friends and see some of my teachers. I found out that one of the guys that I played football with last year, who is a senior this year, had asked Heather to skip school with him."

---

*As men, protection
is part of what we do.*

When Bryan said that, I was outraged. Heather, my sweet daughter. I knew the boy in question. Better yet, I knew this boy's parents, so I decided to immediately get on the telephone. As I began dialing, Bryan said, "Dad, that's not necessary. I took care of it. Let's just put it this way: He will never do that again."

My wife is very nonviolent, and she was upset about what Bryan may have done. I must admit that I didn't question him as to what he did; I just looked him in the eye and asked, "Are you sure you took care of it?" He said he did, and he must have. The boy never again suggested such a thing to my daughter.

One morning when Bryndan and Holly were both in elementary school, they were standing at the bus stop waiting for the school bus. For no apparent reason, a boy about Bryndan's age—three years older than Holly—hit Holly with a stick. She began to cry. Bryndan's immediate reaction was to hit the boy. In fact, he knocked him down and told him to never put his hands on his sister again.

Little did we know that was going to be quite the incident. The youngster went home and told his mother only part of the story, that Bryndan had beat him up. Bryndan really didn't beat him up. As we found out, he just hit the boy one time and the boy fell down. Still, the boy's mother came by our house the following evening complaining that Bryndan had beat up her son. Once Holly told the truth about what had happened, the boy's mother was very, very embarrassed, and so was I. I told her, "We don't approve of violence at all. But your son, who's much bigger than our little girl, hit her with that stick. Bryndan had no recourse but to protect his sister. He was not only doing what was natural, he was doing what I, as his father, expected him to do."

THE SCOPE OF PROTECTION

I don't want to end this chapter with your thinking that I'm promoting violence. In fact, we have taught our children that people are just too violent in our culture, and violence is not the best way to respond to conflict. There are other ways of protecting those who are close to you. The principle that I *do* want to underscore is that, as men, protection is part of what we do. We ought to be willing to risk all that we have, including our own lives if necessary, to protect our families and those who are counting on us.

I care about my kids' physical, moral, and spiritual safety.

The text of 1 Peter 5:1–3 includes a broader issue that goes far beyond physical protection. The bulk of protection is over the minds and souls of those committed to our care. In our household, we're selective about what movies we attend, what videos we rent, what TV shows we watch. We are also careful about what music family members listen to. But it's not enough to just say "don't" once kids are teenagers. You probably know a lot of horror stories about "Christian" students who become atheists in college, daughters who get pregnant as soon as they leave their parents' houses, sons who end up in jail to the embarrassment of their families. These kids have never made their parents' standards their own, and some other influence in their lives proves stronger than the whisper of their parents' voices on their conscience.

So once in a while when we are in the car, I turn to one of those popular radio stations with lyrics that I could never approve of, I listen to a few songs with my children, and together we evaluate the words. I'm cementing the family standards in their minds, moving them from obeying just because I said so to understanding and thinking through moral principles on their own. In a word, I'm protecting their minds by teaching them.

As my father did, I interview young men interested in taking out one of my daughters. That is also an issue of protection, and my daughters know that I do it because I care about my kids' physical, moral, and spiritual safety. A father's protection in several crucial areas is critical to his children's normal, secure development.

Questions and Application

1. What can you do to help your family feel more secure? In what ways do you protect your family now?

2. How do you expect your children to deal with conflict? How have you advised them to deal with playground bullies, for instance?

3. Take a moment to jot down practical things you expect your children to do to protect each other and themselves. Discuss those expectations with your kids soon.

PART FOUR

OUT OF INTEGRITY COMES YOUR INHERITANCE

CHAPTER TEN

MENTOR
COURAGE

"You will have to fight me."

I have a hard time growing grass in our backyard. No matter what I do it, seems that the grass will only grow to a certain point and then wither and die. The problem is obvious. We simply have too many trees in our backyard. There's too much shade, and the sunlight and water don't reach the soil the way they need to. The grass is undernourished, so it dies. I know what I have to do. I have to cut down some of those trees and trim back the branches on the others so that the natural elements can get to the ground, nourish that grass, and cause it to grow.

In much the same way, allowing our kids to be exposed to the world around them is part of the role of parents. I know I said in the previous chapter that one of our great roles is to protect our children. But, paradoxically, another role is to *release* them; to grant and give them the courage to face the challenges of life.

Our kids need to be exposed to life's elements. We do

them a great disservice when, in the name of developing them, we overprotect them. Protection is not development. Part of development is exposure, and our kids need to learn how to take a few hits so that their courage is strengthened. Courage is a product of persevering and being diligent in the midst of adverse circumstances. Controlling our kids' environment does not necessarily equip them for the challenges of the real world. Look at it this way: A ship is safe in harbor, but that's not what it was built for. Sooner or later it must set sail. We need to make sure that the "little ships" we send out of the harbors of our homes are seaworthy.

We want them to become salt and light in society rather than having the world become leaven to them.

We all know the stories of kids who live in fine Christian homes, go to wonderful Christian schools, enjoy a nice controlled Christian environment, and tragically end up shipwrecked. Perhaps they go off to a secular university. Maybe they encounter a mainstream workplace. But because they have lived in a cocoon, insulated from some of the hard knocks of life and from the realities of the sinful world in which we live, they are overwhelmed by what they face. Now don't get me wrong, please. We need to give our children a moral and biblical foundation from which they can draw upon biblical solutions to the challenges that face them. I am not saying that we should overexpose our kids to negative experiences in life. A person doesn't have to experience everything to know some things are wrong.

Still, I think there is an overreaction in the Christian culture, particularly when it comes to rearing our kids, that often does the opposite of what we want. Our chosen culture can remove our children so far from the realities of life that, oddly enough, they're not able to handle the avalanche of temptations and pressure when suddenly immersed in it. Rather than keep our children entirely insulated, it is better to incrementally expose them to the sinful realities of this world so that they can build appropriate responses and develop corresponding toughness. We want them to own their relationship with Christ and internalize and incorporate truth into the realities of life. We want them to become salt and light in society rather than having the world become leaven to them. In order to do that, they have to develop courage.

PREPARING KIDS TO
FACE MORAL CHALLENGES

I believe my father intuitively understood this. He wouldn't necessarily articulate it this way, but Pop knew that he would not be around all our lives. He knew that there would be a time that each of his children needed to move on and establish their own lives, ready to face the challenges of life around them. Pop understood that if he bailed us out of every situation, rushed in to take the heat for us, or picked up the boxing gloves on our behalf whenever we had a hassle, then he was not encouraging courage but rather entrenching us in weakness and dependency. He understood that we couldn't live life effectively if we reacted out of fear and were easily intimidated by the challenges of life.

FIGHT HIM OR FIGHT ME

In the early 1960s, the central ward of Newark was a very

tough place to live. During the first ten years of my life, 1950 to 1960, family values permeated our working-class community. There was a sense of warmth in the neighborhood; everybody watched out for everybody else. But around 1960, the community and the neighborhood began to take a nosedive. We saw it in the schools first. More and more kids were a little hardened and tough. There were more fights. The moral fiber of the community began to crack and to erode.

In the school year 1961–62, I was in the seventh grade. I had the uncomfortable experience of being the youngest in my class because I had skipped the sixth grade. When I entered Central Avenue Middle School, not only was I the youngest, but I was also feeling intimidated because this was a new school and it had kids I didn't know. Only a few of my friends came to this school. I felt like a fish out of water.

A kid in our class, Jimmy, was a "seventh-grade terrorist." He personified the word *bully*. Because I had skipped a grade and Jimmy had been kept back a grade, Jimmy was a couple of years older than I. Thankfully, he wasn't much bigger than I was, since I was fairly big for my age.

Jimmy picked on me constantly. He'd do little things like knock my books out of my hand. Often when I walked to school, I'd run into Jimmy. He'd make fun of me and shove me around. Jimmy tried to bully me and take money from me. Pop had some strong rules about not picking fights, so I structured my day to avoid Jimmy.

I told Mom about the situation. She made a beeline to the school and talked to the principal about it, much to my embarrassment. Jimmy was warned, but nothing changed. It was getting a little bit ridiculous.

Because my dad worked nights, often he had left for work by the time I came in from school. One weekend, though, he said to me, "Your mother's been telling me that this little boy's been picking on you and that you've been complaining about it. You know, Son, you're going to have to stand up to this boy. This stuff has to stop. I don't want you running from this kid anymore. I don't want you being intimidated by him again. He has to learn his lesson, that he can't put his hands on you. Now if you keep letting him put his hands on you, you keep letting him push you around, then he's just going to constantly pick on you and the rest of the kids are going to think that you are an easy target. Son, I want this to stop."

Then he gave me a directive I'll never forget as he looked into my eyes, put his hand on my shoulder, and said, "C. W." (my childhood nickname), "if this boy terrorizes you or puts his hand on you one more time and you don't fight him back, then you will have to fight me." Pop understood we did not live in a perfect world. He wanted us to get along with others, but he knew that was not always possible and sometimes we needed to defend ourselves. He didn't want me hurt, but he didn't want me responding like a coward, either.

I knew Pop wasn't joking when he said that. He had that very serious look about him, and I knew I had no other choice. I could either just keep my mouth shut and take it from Jimmy and then deal with Pop, or I could stand up to Jimmy.

Monday came after the weekend right on schedule. I didn't sleep at all on Sunday night because I knew that Jimmy, in typical fashion, would see me and do something to terrorize me. He might slap me upside my head or knock my books down, and I would once again be the laughingstock of Central Avenue Middle School.

This Monday, however, Jimmy didn't bother me the whole school day. But after school, Jimmy was waiting for me as I walked out of the school door onto the playground. Sure enough, he came up to me and pushed me. At that point, my father's words echoed in my mind: "If you don't fight this boy, you will have to fight me."

I slammed my books down and I screamed at him, "Jimmy, no more. You're not going to put your hands on me anymore. I'm tired of this." We began to square off. I put my hands up and prepared to do what needed to be done. My heart was pounding a thousand times per minute because I knew Jimmy might pulverize me. Then the miracle of miracles happened. Jimmy laughed, backed off, and walked away. You know what? The kid never bothered me again. He was a typical bully. Bullies are usually more talk and intimidation than they are action.

> *We want our children to know*
> *that whatever God says is certain.*

TEACHING THE PRINCIPLE OF COURAGE

Would my dad have told me to do it that way today? Probably not. You see, back in the fifties and early sixties when kids had a fistfight, that's exactly what it was: a fistfight. There weren't guns and knives, at least not in our school. Would I tell my kids to handle situations that way? No. In fact, I've told my kids, my boys especially, to try to walk away from physical conflict. I've instructed them to protect themselves but to remember that kids are really violent these days. There are other ways of handling things, but the principle that my dad taught me was right. He knew that if I started running, then perhaps I would develop a habit of always running whenever I faced opposition. Pop didn't want me to become a coward. He knew that I was going to have a family one day and that I would have to take care of them and protect them. In a word, he was mentoring courage.

But he didn't stop with teaching me to be courageous in areas of physical danger. He taught moral courage. He taught his kids to be honest when we had blown it. He taught us to look people in the eye and tell the truth.

I believe that part of the reason for the dearth of leadership today is that we men have grown up in families where fathers did not help their children to live life courageously. Part of being a man from a biblical perspective is learning how to face your fears, to walk right toward them, and to do what is right in light of opposition. That's really all that courage is about.

UNDERSTANDING BIBLICAL COURAGE

Joshua 1:1-9 is a biblical exposition on courage. Let's look at this text.

Now it came about after the death of Moses the servant of the Lord that the Lord spoke to Joshua the son of Nun, Moses' servant, saying, "Moses My servant is dead; now therefore arise, cross this Jordan, you and all this people, to the land which I am giving to them, to the sons of Israel. Every place on which the sole of your foot treads, I have given it to you, just as I spoke to Moses. From the wilderness and this Lebanon, even as far as the great river, the river Euphrates, all the land of the Hittites, and as far as the Great Sea toward the setting of the sun, will be your territory. No man will be able to stand before you all the days of your life. Just as I have been with Moses, I will be with you; I will not fail you or forsake you. Be strong and courageous, for you shall give this people possession of the land which I swore to their fathers to give them. Only be strong and very courageous; be careful to do according to all the law which Moses My servant commanded you; do not turn from it to the right

141

or to the left, so that you may have success wherever you go. This book of the law shall not depart from your mouth, but you shall meditate on it day and night, so that you may be careful to do according to all that is written in it; for then you will make your way prosperous, and then you will have success. Have I not commanded you? Be strong and courageous! Do not tremble or be dismayed, for the Lord your God is with you wherever you go."

Courage rises out of the context of challenge.

A Clear Assignment from God

In times of great challenge, I've often gone to this passage to receive the motivation and encouragement I need to keep moving in the midst of troubled waters. There seems to be a four-part descriptive definition concerning courage in this text. First, *courage rests upon a clear assignment from God.* In verses 1–3, God reminded Joshua that Moses, the great lawgiver, was dead. The assignment for leading the people of Israel now rested upon Joshua's shoulders. Then God specifically told Joshua what he needed to do: He had to get up, cross over the Jordan River, and go occupy the land. Although the details of the assignment are not spelled out yet, no one can doubt the clarity of direction God gave him. Joshua was now God's chosen leader, and he had a task that needed to be done.

Truly courageous action is not just a matter of doing whatever you want to do or responding to situations, but a positive response to a clear sense of direction. This is especially true for those of us who have a relationship with Christ. This applies to how we lead our homes too. We are not telling our kids simply to do things that we want them to do, but we are helping them to embrace God's truth and God's direction in order to face the challenges of life. We want our children to know that whatever God says is certain, despite the intimidating voices of the culture in which we live.

An Assurance of God's Presence

Second, *courage rests upon the assurance of God's presence.* In both verse 5 and verse 9, God says to Joshua that He will be with him. A number of years ago, I did a study of the callings of God to service throughout the Bible. To my amazement, I discovered that there is never a call from God that does not include the assurance of His presence. God never gives us an assignment without going with us; we can rely upon Him. Part of our role as fathers as we nurture our children is not only to point them to the assignment and to tell them to listen to God for their direction, but it is also to let them know that they never face life alone. They need to know that one with God is always a majority. The more confidence that we can give them in the God of the ages, the more clearly we point them to God's unfailing track record in their lives, the more they will be able to face the opposition and challenges of life with courage.

A Focused Determination

Third, *courage rests upon a focused determination.* Three times in these verses God tells Joshua to be strong and courageous. Take note of that. God commands Joshua to be strong and courageous. Courage is not necessarily the product of a personality type but, as this text demonstrates, courage is a product of acting courageously. In other words, we become how we behave. God told Joshua, "Now look, buddy, these people on the other side of the river won't warmly welcome you as you take their land and their houses. There *will* be opposition."

In fact, there is no such thing as courage unless there is opposition. There's no such thing as courage unless there's a challenge. Courage rises out of the context of challenge. It shows itself in contrast to the context of doom and devastation and failure. Those who make a determination not to go with the flow, but to stand against the flow, will stand out as being courageous. Act courageously, God said to Joshua. You can't wimp out. Don't cave in to the pressures around you. Don't listen to the voices of despair around you. You know what the assignment is. I've already told you that I'm going to be with you; now it's your turn. *You* act courageously. *You* act upon the assurances that I've given to you.

A Biblical Perspective

Fourth, *courage rests upon a biblical perspective.* In verse 8, God said clearly to Joshua that the success of his mission hinged on his commitment to biblical truth. If Joshua would live his life according to the word of God, God said that He would underscore and put exclamation marks around what Joshua did. I can't emphasize this principle enough: Our kids are not to live their lives based upon stories and illustrations alone, or great warm fuzzies and nice family traditions. That won't get them far at all, other than making books of memories. Our kids need to live their lives based upon truth. At every turn in their lives, we need to point them to timeless truth. We need to point them back to the Word of God because at the moment of their crisis, that's where they will have to return to gain the strength to keep on moving.

That's what God was telling Joshua: "Joshua, your father

in ministry, your great mentor, Moses, is gone. But his influence on your life lives on. You've got to take what I taught him and said to him via My word and through the experiences he had with Me. Now it's your turn to apply them. If you live consistently in the light of what I say in this book, then I will bless your life in ways that you never dreamed possible."

Our children must learn to look their fear in the eye and keep moving toward God.

Pop's commitment to God was a quiet one. He insisted his family attend church and he lived his life based on scriptural principles. But I don't have memories of seeing him spend hours on his knees before sunrise or his calling us together for daily family devotions. He didn't always tell us the biblical reason behind what he told us to do. In fact, my mother was a little more involved in our day-to-day spiritual training. But the consistency of both their lives was noteworthy. For some reason, after we kids left home, his more visible spiritual life blossomed. But even while we were under his roof, he taught us by his example how to follow Christ courageously.

I love how Dan Hayes, the director of Atlanta Community Ministries and a great friend of mine, defines courage: "Courage is not the absence of fear, but courage is the ability to do that which you fear." That's what we are trying to teach our kids, isn't it? We want them not to allow fear to imprison them and then cause them to shrink back, but we want them to be able to hear God's clear voice, to see His direction and, despite what anybody else says, to take courageous steps forward. Our children must learn to look their fear in the eye and keep moving toward God.

ALLOWING KIDS' MORAL MUSCLES TO DEVELOP

The first practical way to help our kids embrace this perspective is to resist the temptation of controlling their lives, solving their problems, and fighting their battles for them. As I said before, protection is not necessarily development. Many times as a father I've had to swallow hard and to resist my own temptation to help my kids out of tough situations.

During our older daughter Heather's freshman year in college, she had a roommate whose lifestyle and morals were inconsistent with the biblical values we had passed along to our daughter. Heather called home the first week she was at school and told us what was happening in her own dorm room. My first inclination was to get in my car, drive to the school, and handle that problem quickly for Heather. But as I considered doing that, I thought, *No, now is exam time. It's time for Heather to tell us what she thinks she should do in light of this opposition.* We let Heather resolve the situation. She chose to talk with the roommate and then to move out. I must say she passed that "exam time" with flying colors.

When our son Bryan was away at college, an incident took place on campus that, according to his report to me, seemed like a terrible injustice. Because I knew the president of the school, I asked Bryan, "Son, do you want me to call the president to get some action on this matter?" I was ready to do it, but his response helped me to understand that was not appropriate.

He simply said to me, "Now, Dad, you know I'm old

enough to handle some of these things myself. I'll take care of it."

I humbly bowed my head, realizing that I'd just gotten my parental hand slapped. I said, "Son, you're right—and you're learning your lessons well."

It's a delicate balance between protection and exposure, but it's a balance worth pursuing. Teaching our children courage today will develop them into the Joshuas of tomorrow.

Questions and Application

1. What are three things you can do to teach your children courage?
2. Think of your family history. Are there examples of courage among your relatives and/or family friends? Tell them to your children.
3. What are the fears your children face today? Talk with them and find out, then pray with them for God's help as they face them.

CHAPTER ELEVEN

IDENTIFY FENCES

"This is my house."

When Bryan was about eleven, he went through what I call "the 'that's not fair' phase." It seemed that any time Karen and I asked him to do something, he responded with his patented statement, "That's not fair." We put up with it for a while but then, quite frankly, it began to irritate me. Finally I had had enough. Bryan wanted to go someplace with a friend. We didn't feel as if Bryan should go. When I told him I wasn't going to let him go, he looked at me and said, "Dad, that's not fair."

I said, "Son, come here. Let me tell you what time of day it is. It seems that every time we've told you something lately, you turn around and tell us that it's not fair. Well, life isn't fair. It's time you realized that you can't live life based upon what's fair and what's not fair, but upon what is right." And then I added this line: "Now, Son, I know that in school you are studying democracy. That's how this country runs. But let me tell you the difference between our house and the rest of the United States of America. This country is a democracy. People vote on politicians and whoever wins the election is placed in office. Our household is not a democracy. Our household is a benevolent dictatorship, and if you keep pushing the limits, I'm going to drop the benevolent part." He seemed to get the message.

ORDER IN THE HOME

My kids will tell you that I'm a teddy bear. My bark is worse than my bite. Karen and I try to say yes more than we say no, but there are times in life when a parent has to say no. If, as a parent, you are afraid to say no, you're in big trouble. "No" can be one of the most positive words in the English language, for the word "no" helps us to be able to point our kids in the right direction and to have them appreciate choices in life. There cannot be order and direction in the house if all the members of the household do whatever they want, whenever they want to do it. "No" becomes a valuable ally in reining people in, not to hurt them, but to give some sense of orderly direction to the home. Note that that also includes the adults saying no to some of their desires too. If you expect more discipline from your kids than you are able to show, they will sense it and resent it.

In 1 Timothy 3:4, the apostle Paul lists the duties of overseers and deacons in the church. He makes an interesting statement that I believe can be applied to anybody in a position of leadership, especially those of us who are fathers: "He must be one who manages his own household well, keeping his children under control with all dignity." This passage is not teaching that you can guarantee your children will turn out to be balanced, godly members of society. Neither is it teaching that your children will never disobey or rebel against you. You know better than that. Karen and I have known wonderful, godly couples through the years whose hearts have been right. They've done things by the book, and yet their children decide to rebel, reject the faith, and live lives that are in direct contradiction to their upbringing. I don't believe that you can guarantee how your kids will turn out.

However, the emphasis in this text is that a child should never be allowed to permanently disrupt the order and moral direction of the household while living in that home. Dad is in charge of maintaining order. Weak parents, by caving in to the whims and wishes of their kids, allow their kids to manipulate the household and create all kinds of chaos at home. Some dads allow their children to run roughshod over their wives. In the name of "love," children are allowed to do or say whatever they want. That's not right. I realize that hyperactivity and Attention Deficit Disorder are realities. But I also know these labels are used to sanitize the condition of many kids who are just out of control. In these cases, the child is not hyperactive or really suffering from ADD. Parents are just afraid to rein him in and to do whatever it takes to build some strong fences and boundaries to check his behavior.

As in most things, Pop had a very simple, straightforward view on this. He'd say, "Any child that I feed, clothe, provide shelter for, and care for will listen to me and abide by the rules of this house." Pop meant that. As we got older, we clearly knew what the alternative was—homelessness. At critical points of disagreements, he would sometimes look at us and say, "Well, this *is* my house." Pop never understood how a parent could say, "I can't do anything with this child of mine."

THE LIGHT TOUCH

Pop had a great sense of humor, though. When I was a teenager I would sometimes say to him with a smile, "Pop, I'm going to do whatever I want to do." And he would look at me and then he would look up at the ceiling and look back at me and half-jokingly say, "Son, you can do whatever you want to do, but you're just not going to do it here."

For life to be full and joyful,
there must be limits and boundaries.

Pop was not some dictator who took great delight in spitting out orders, or someone who was so controlling and needy that he had to remind everybody, including himself, who was in charge. In fact, he very seldom reminded anybody who was in charge. The man who constantly goes around the house saying "This is my house!" is probably not sure that he is the head of the house and that the house really belongs to him.

Pop had relatively few rules and he gave us plenty of latitude. He loved to laugh and kid with us. He could take it as well as dish it out. He never took himself too seriously. In fact, I think sometimes my mother was a little tighter than Pop was on the day-to-day issues.

THE BIG THREE

Pop never had a bunch of nitpicky rules around the house, but he was determined that there was going to be order and direction in his home. Really, he only had three big rules. I call them "The Three Ds": He would not tolerate outright disobedience, dishonesty, or disrespect. If a child of his violated any one of these three, there was no negotiation, there was no compromise. That child was a candidate for immediate, decisive discipline at the mercy of Crawford W. Loritts, Sr. I remember him telling me when I was young, "Now, Son, when you lie"—and it's interesting that he didn't say "if you lie"; he knew part of human nature was to lie— "boy, when you lie to me, you'd better tell the best lie you ever told in your life." My sisters and I were scared spitless to lie to Pop. I'm not saying we didn't do it, but we were just petrified to lie to him.

In a strange sense, it gave us a great deal of comfort and freedom knowing where the boundaries were in our household. As fathers we frustrate our children when we aren't clear about what the rules of the household are and what is expected of family members. You think about that for a second. One of the most frustrating things in the world is not to know what's expected of you on the job. It's the same thing for our children at home. We must use discipline and orderliness to help our children understand their roles. It's not that you're being mean to your kids; you are helping them to understand that for life to be full and joyful, there must be limits and boundaries. You are helping them to become productive members of society, beginning at home.

This was true in the house I grew up in, even as we grew older. We were reminded that since we lived at Mom and Pop's house, we had certain responsibilities. We had to contribute to the household and to abide by the rules. Even when I went off to college and came back home, there were certain household rules. If I ate there or slept there, then there would be certain things that I needed to do, even as an adult visiting there. When I came home, my father would jokingly remind me, "This is still my house." Good humor or not, there is an inescapable sense of responsibility when you live in community with other people.

Pop also taught us to respect and abide by the rules of other people when we were visiting someone else's home. He reminded us to make sure that we didn't violate the direction of that household. It was important to respect the boundaries of other people, even though I might not personally embrace them. When we visited at relatives' or friends' houses, I had to ask permission to eat in rooms other than the dining room or the kitchen or play in certain areas. It was my job to find out the household boundaries and abide by them. "All right, you're under their authority" was what he'd tell me when I was heading out to stay with an aunt and uncle for a week or two.

COMMUNITY RESPONSIBILITY

When Bryan and Heather went off to college and came back, they had some adjustments to go through. Because they had been away from home, they had enjoyed certain freedoms. Even though they were growing up, there were certain basic rules of the household they still had to respect. For example, our kids know that they do not just go out and stay out as long as they want to. They may stay out for a while, but they need to call in to let us know where they are. I tell them that even though I'm the head of the house, I still call in. I don't "just go out." "Out" has an address, after all.

Boundaries need to be firmly established, particularly as it relates to how things are done in my house.

It's not that we're trying to control their lives; it's simply a part of living in the Loritts community and being responsible. When we drove Bryan home at the end of his first year in college and we pulled up into the driveway at home, I noticed the grass needed to be cut. I had something else to do and I said to Bryan, "Son, I'd like for you to cut the grass for me."

He half-jokingly replied, "Oh, Dad, I don't do grass."

I quickly responded, "Well, Son, do you do college?"

He said, "Oh, yeah, that's right, Dad. OK, I'll get the lawn mower." Since I was still paying the freight, I assumed that if he wanted to eat and live at my house that he would cut a few blades of grass.

EXPECTING RESPECT

Once a contractor came to our house to give us a bid on an addition. We were sitting around the kitchen table examining his proposal, and our two younger children were not too far away from us in the dining room. I told him that because there was a considerable sum of money involved, Karen and I would have to take his proposal, talk about it, and then call him back in a few days. I don't know what got into him, but this particular contractor became very forceful and disrespectful toward both Karen and me. He looked at me and basically said I was a liar. He said "No, you're not going to do that. That's what they all say."

I responded, "Sir, I am not perfect. I'm sure that there are a lot of inadequacies in my own life, but lying is not one of my faults. I don't appreciate that statement." Out of the corner of my eye, I saw my two younger children just looking up as if to say, *Oh, man, what's going to happen next?*

Then this gentleman turned to Karen and said, "Well, I heard from him. What do you have to say about this?" His voice was very offensive and disrespectful. He said a couple of other things to my wife and I stopped him.

"Hold it, sir. This is my house. You are a visitor in my home, and this is our money that we are talking about. Not only that, but I don't talk to my wife that way and there's not a man in the world I will allow to talk to her that way. Gather up all of your stuff and get out of my house." I escorted him to the door. My kids saw that.

I felt very bad about having to end that discussion in that manner. But my son just put his arm over my shoulder and said, "Dad, he doesn't understand who he's talking to." Now I'm nobody. I don't consider myself anyone special. It was regrettable that I had to do that, but boundaries need to be firmly established, particularly as it relates to how things are done in my house.

While the man was making those disrespectful comments toward Karen and me, I could hear my father's voice whispering in my ear, "This is my house." It helped me remember that there really *is* a difference between my house and the rest of the United States of America.

Questions and Application

1. What are some things you do to let your children know that you expect them to honor your spouse?

2. Do you ever feel as though your efforts at discipline in your house are spent too much on "nitpicky" things, and not enough in making sure the big ground rules are understood? If so, talk it over with your spouse. See if there are "nitpicky" things that can be de-emphasized in favor of focusing your efforts on "the big stuff," and develop an action plan to make it happen.

3. Take three sessions to develop a list of "house rules"—one on your own, one with your spouse, and one with your family. Compare and discuss the lists with your family, then develop a master list so your house rules are clearly understood by everyone in your family.

CHAPTER TWELVE

PRACTICE ACCOUNTABILITY

"Do right."

Accountability preserves integrity. Those who never develop an internal sense of accountability have a struggle making objective, right, moral choices in life. Accountability is to character what an architect's blueprints are to a building. The building progresses according to design, and the finished product is the fulfillment of the vision. But along the way there are checks and corrections against a blueprint. That's called accountability.

Because we are imperfect, fallen creatures, we do not naturally gravitate toward right choices. Left to our own devices, we will mess up. We are "prone to wander," as the old hymn says. For our own protection, we must run to accountability and not from it. The quickest road to character demise and moral catastrophe is withdrawal from accountability and isolation from those who love us and are concerned about our development.

Individuals and organizations stunt their development

and even destroy themselves by a lack of accountability. During the past few years, I have read three books about the downfall of Jim Bakker and the PTL ministry (two by Richard Dortch and Jim Bakker's book *I Was Wrong*). Although there were any number of factors contributing to the disintegration of PTL, I was overwhelmed by one frightening observation. PTL collapsed because things got out of hand. The "horses ran wild" and, at critical points, no one could round them up and put them back in the corral. In other words, there was no accountability, so, as the saying goes, the rest is history.

I suppose I could give an encyclopedia of illustrations on the results of the lack of accountability. You know them well. Our prisons are full of people who were not accountable. Families and marriages are destroyed because people are not accountable. We have lost confidence in our community leaders and elected officials because some of them have spurned accountability, and the list goes on.

FORMING A SENSE OF ACCOUNTABILITY

Since accountability preserves integrity, where is accountability framed and formed? I believe that the need for accountability must be branded on the souls of children as soon as possible by their parents. In fact, I don't think it's stretching it to say that "accountability" is an excellent synonym for "parenting."

My father had a very strong sense as to what was right and what was wrong. He really believed that we ought to live our lives based upon what we knew to be right. He expected that our behavior would measure up to those things that were objectively right and that we would walk away from those things that were wrong. That was Pop's simple approach to things. This was often reinforced in my teen years. You know how it is with teenagers; at that stage we feel as if our perspectives are just as good as our parents', sometimes better than theirs. We feel as if our parents are a little bit out of touch. We feel like we can chart our own course because we know more than our parents do. I didn't escape that mind-set. I was a little bit headstrong. Thankfully, Pop was wise and, although he emphasized accountability, he wasn't into controlling our lives.

I am responsible for what I do.
Nobody else is.

There's a difference between accountability and control. Pop knew that at certain points in our development we needed to internally embrace the difference between right and wrong. Often, when I was a teenager on my way to go out, my father wasn't really sure about what I might be "getting into." So he would say these words to me just before I would go out: "Do right. Son, do right." I still remember the feeling I had when Pop looked me in the eye as I was getting ready to leave and said, "Boy, do right." I can't tell you the number of times that expression bailed me out of some potentially devastating situations when I could have compromised my behavior or done something that would have brought shame to myself and my family. It was much later on, when I was well into adulthood, that I told Pop about the impact of those words on me.

The expression "do right" was Pop's way of letting me know that he trusted me, but also it was a warning not to violate that trust. It was precisely because he trusted his kids that we did not want to do anything that would bring shame to our family. "Do right" was based on our relationship with Pop—and that's the key. It wasn't a legalistic statement or some little reminder that he had a billy club waiting to clobber us if we messed up (although if we did mess up, we'd have to pay the consequences). As I look back over it, it was more a summary statement of his love and commitment to us. It was as if Pop were saying, "Son, I have given myself to you and you know how I've tried to behave around you. You know about my love for you and the amount of time that I've spent with you. I am releasing you to uncertain situations, and now you are being tested to see if you are going to act in accordance with everything that has been deposited in you."

TRANSFERRING RESPONSIBILITY

Although he wasn't highly educated in the formal sense, in many ways my father was an extremely wise man. You see, Pop understood that maturity meant transferring the responsibility for my behavior to me as soon as I could handle it. That's what he meant by "do right." He was telling me I was responsible for my behavior and its consequences. In those two words, he was saying, "Boy, I don't know exactly where you are going and I don't know what you'll be doing every moment, but you're at an age right now where I must increase the level of my trust in you. So now you're responsible for your own choices and your own behavior."

What Does "Do Right" Mean?

As I look back, I think Pop was telling me at least four things when he used those two words, "do right." First, he was saying *he wanted me to behave the way I was taught.* "Do right" was the rewind mechanism in the videotape of what Pop had taught us. "Do right" said, "OK, roll that tape back and don't get a case of character amnesia on me when you are out there this evening. Don't draw a curtain around your background. Don't go out and willfully ignore what has been deposited in your life." "Do right" was Pop's way of saying, "Remember the way you were taught, remember what has been invested in your life, and be sure that you make your choices based upon what you have learned."

> *I'm not going to trespass that which I've been taught, and I'm not going to violate trust to have a good time.*

The second thing that I think he was saying to me was to *own my behavior.* I am responsible for what I do. Nobody else is; I own that. My behavior is not determined by my environment or my friends. I am in control of myself. Whatever I choose to do, I am responsible for those choices. Pop really fought the influence of peer pressure by teaching us that we should not allow anything in society to determine what is morally right or wrong for us. Neither should we do anything just because our friends do. Pop always encouraged us to choose our friends wisely. He put it like this: "Son, you hang out with people that are going somewhere and want to do something with their lives." Pop wasn't talking about being arrogant and snooty, but he made clear that he preferred that we associate with folks whose behavior agreed with what we had been taught. He understood quite clearly that in one sense, we might become who we associate with.

On the other hand, he didn't want us making excuses about our activities. If we found ourselves in a place where everybody else was doing an undesirable thing, Pop expected us not to get involved with it. His directions were simple: You can always walk away. You can always leave them where they are. You don't have to be like that. Pop gave us heavy doses of the strength of character. Character is stronger than environment.

The third thing that Pop was saying when he said "Do right" was that *character is what you do in the dark when nobody is watching you.* He was saying that I had the opportunity to prove I was the man I'd been telling him I was. I had the opportunity to prove that I was as mature and grown as I'd been telling the rest of the family. Since I was so grown, since I felt as if I could control my life, and since I knew what to do and how to act, I had the opportunity to prove it, not so much to Pop as to myself and those I was going to be with.

Even from his grave,
Pop holds me accountable.

Finally, I think he was saying that *self-control is the issue.* Pop knew that having fun doesn't mean you're out of control. But "do right" means there's a line that you won't cross, that you have to make up your mind to say, "I'm only going to go so far. I'm not going to violate my integrity, I'm not going to trespass that which I've been taught, and I'm not going to violate trust to have a good time. I'm not going to sneak around and do things that I know are really wrong that might cause people who are committed to me to be ashamed." It was an issue of controlling one's behavior. Let yourself and others around know how far you are going to go.

Have I always done right? Absolutely not. I'm a sinner just like everyone else. Sadly, there have been times in my life where I have fumbled the ball. I've had to repent, and God has mercifully forgiven me. But my dad's expression, "do right," is with me to this very day. I suppose that has served as one of the motivating factors for me to pray a special prayer through the years. I began praying this when I was in my early twenties, just beginning in ministry. I've prayed throughout the years that before I would do anything that would bring reproach and shame on the name of Christ, on my family, on the ministry that He's given me, and on the people who have been committed to me, that God would take me home to be with Him. That attitude can be directly traced to the work of Christ in my own heart and life and also to Pop.

It's really something how many times a day I think about Pop saying to me "Do right" when I am presented with an "opportunity" to compromise. When I want to retaliate against someone who I feel has done something wrong, and I want to treat the person in the way he has treated me, I can hear my dad saying to me, "Boy, do right. Do right." Even from his grave, Pop holds me accountable.

Other Forces Holding Us Accountable

For those of us who are Christians, God has given us not only parents as an outside force to hold us accountable, but He has also given us Himself, His Word, and fellow believers to hold us accountable so that we keep moving in God's direction with our choices and behavior in life. The Word of God is full of instruction on responsibility, living in community with one another, and our behavioral choices. One of the classic texts on accountability and integrity is Psalm 15. I would encourage every father to make this a primary text that he teaches his children throughout the course of their development. Dads could also take this on as a challenge to measure up to the character traits that David outlines in this psalm.

> O Lord, who may abide in Thy tent?
> Who may dwell on Thy holy hill?
> He who walks with integrity, and works righteousness,
> And speaks truth in his heart.
> He does not slander with his tongue,
> Nor does evil to his neighbor,
> Nor takes up a reproach against his friend;
> In whose eyes a reprobate is despised,
> But who honors those who fear the Lord;
> He swears to his own hurt, and does not change;
> He does not put out his money at interest,
> Nor does he take a bribe against the innocent.
> He who does these things will never be shaken.

Did you notice that last sentence? "He who does these things will never be shaken." I really believe that this is a statement concerning the strength of character. The one who walks with integrity will have depth and strength of character. This person will not be easily swayed by the winds and currents of the culture, by the fads and forms of society. In contrast, this one will bring to life a sense of direction. He will become a visible model of the transforming power of Christ in the context of his environment at his point in history. She will become an inviting alternative to her generation because she is what she proclaims. They will become living models of the grace of God and the strength of God because they have chosen the path of accountability and integrity.

Who You Are, Not Just What You Do

Just as my dad planted the seed of accountability and integrity in my soul, Karen and I have a burning desire that our children don't just "accomplish things" in life, but that they become Christlike and godly throughout the course of their lives. Every day of their lives I want our kids to understand that *who they are is far more important than what they accomplish.*

---

*Character determines behavior
no matter what one's environment
or circumstances may be.*

Our older son is involved in ministry now, and he's in graduate school. When we talk on the phone, I'm forever asking him questions about his walk with God, his devotional life, and his own personal development. I rejoice with him about his great accomplishments and the gifts that God has given him, particularly as a communicator, but we've had even better discussions about erasing the line between what we do and what we are.

I have always been the one who takes our children to school. We go through the same routine every morning. After we get in the car, one of the first things we do is to pray about the day. Then as we drive the few miles from our house to the schools that they attend, we talk about their plans for the day. When I drop them off, I make three statements (usually they finish them before I do because they know them so well). First, I tell each one of them how much I love them and that I want them to have a great day. Then I say to them, "I want you to remember who you are today." Finally I tell them, "Make a difference with your life today. This school ought to be different for the honor and glory of God because you were there."

The reason I tell them that is twofold: First, if they remember who they are, they will not be so swayed by what others say they ought to be. I want them to have a strong sense that they have been created in the image of God, that they are loved, that they have come from somewhere. They need to remember the people who love them and have invested in their lives because, you see, I believe that character determines behavior no matter what one's environment or circumstances may be. I want them to understand that.

Second, I want my kids to have a sense of mission. They need to know that they can make a difference. They're not in school just to learn, just to have fun, or just to be with their friends. God has them there because, not only have they come from somewhere, but they are going somewhere. I want them to understand, even at a young age, that they are pilgrims and strangers in this world. As such, they have to live life with purpose and intention.

REPRESENTING GOD
AND MAKING A DIFFERENCE

I really believe that once you understand where you came from and where you are going, an internal sense of accountability arises. If you understand the impact that you are going to have either for good or for evil, that edits out many negatives that will be detrimental to your character development. Far too many parents rear their kids negatively. We give them a list of stuff that they *shouldn't* be doing. Certainly we have to say that from time to time, but whenever we give them a list of what they should not be doing, then what they should not be doing becomes a mission in life. God has something more positive.

God wants our kids to represent Him, to become salt and light in the context of this fallen world, to redeem society. They can be a vehicle through which the love of Jesus Christ can be displayed whether they are students in first grade, seniors in high school, or sophomores in college. Wherever they are in life, they can represent the mission of Christ in the world in which they live. Anywhere our children go, we can help with their behavior because we can always remind them, "God wants you to make a difference with your life." As they mature they begin asking, "How does the choice that I'm making right now contribute to the impact that God wants me to make?"

I say that so often to our children simply because, should I not be there due to my life being (from a human perspective) cut short, at least I want them to know that God has them here for a purpose. I want that on the front burners of their own hearts and lives as soon as possible. That sense of destiny—that they are here for God's purpose—is a part of them. That develops their sense of accountability, so another generation learns what it means to "do right."

Questions and Application

1. What things can you do with your children to encourage them to do right?

2. How often do you verbally encourage your children before you leave them at school or before they leave the house in the morning? How can you help your children prepare to demonstrate the love of Christ to their friends?

TOUCH
YOUR FAMILY

"Son, I love you."

Have you ever thought about the importance and power of a touch? I have been intrigued by the prominence that touch plays in the Bible. For example, there is a *touch of affection*. In Acts 20:36–38, Paul was giving his farewell to the Ephesians. The Ephesians were so moved by their relationship with the apostle that they embraced him and kissed him. They were saddened because they wouldn't see him again.

Then there's the *commissioning touch* mentioned in 1 Timothy 4:14 and 2 Timothy 1:6. Apparently Timothy was somehow intimidated by the church he was leading. He was not exercising his gifts to their fullest potential, and Paul reminded him that he had been approved by the leaders of the church. He challenged the young leader to stir up or rekindle that gift that was given to him by the laying on of hands.

There's also the *touch of affirmation and blessing*. This has to do with initiating a legacy and establishing a destiny, as exemplified in Genesis 48:8–21. In this passage, Jacob blessed Joseph's sons to secure their place in history.

But probably one of the most revealing biblical texts on touch is Mark 5:25–34. Look closely at this passage:

> And a woman who had had a hemorrhage for twelve years, and had endured much at the hands of many physicians, and had spent all that she had and was not helped at all, but rather had grown worse, after hearing about Jesus, came up in the crowd behind Him, and touched His cloak. For she thought, "If I just touch His garments, I shall get well." And immediately the flow of her blood was dried up; and she felt in her body that she was healed of her affliction. And immediately Jesus, perceiving in Himself that the power proceeding from Him had gone forth, turned around in the crowd and said, "Who touched my garments?" And His disciples said to Him, "You see the multitude pressing in on You, and You say, 'Who touched Me?'" And He looked around to see the woman who had done this. But the woman fearing and trembling, aware of what had happened to her, came and fell down before Him, and told Him the whole truth. And He said to her, "Daughter, your faith has made you well; go in peace, and be healed of your affliction."

This passage is pregnant with all sorts of implications. For our purposes, I want to draw attention to the woman's touch. It is obvious from the passage that Jesus was immersed in a swarm of people. They were "pressing against Him," according to the text. Jesus' disciples were amazed that He would raise the question, "Who touched me?" There were a lot of people *handling* Jesus, but evidently only one *touched* Him. He felt the *touch of faith,* and He responded to that touch with healing. It can be said that the woman touched Him and He, in turn, permanently touched her.

COLLARBONE MASSAGES

Note that *to handle is not necessarily to touch.* It all depends on what we are trying to convey when we use our hands, particularly on our children. My father was born February 13, 1914, and thus grew up in the early part of this century. Pop was a child of his generation. In his era, it was not considered appropriate for a man to tell his children, especially his boys, that he loved them. Yet my father said it in scores of ways. In many respects, my dad was a paradox. He was tough and yet he was tender. For whatever reason, he didn't allow himself to verbalize the tender side of his nature. Yet we were constantly aware when we were around him that Pop was a man whose bark often was much worse than his bite.

---

*Pop's hand became
the signature over my soul.*

Some of my most cherished memories are of sitting on my dad's lap as a young boy. In fact, if he was watching a game and I was hanging in the shadow, he would simply grab me and put me up on his lap. Often, when we would be coming back from a baseball game in New York, I would fall asleep on the train with his arm draped over me. Then there were his famous collarbone massages. He loved to rub our collarbones, and I don't mean just when we were kids. Sometimes he would walk past me in the kitchen and briefly rub my collarbone, or if I sat next to him watching TV, he would give me the old collarbone touch. I guess it was his way of saying, "I love you. I would rather be with my family than with anyone else. You matter to me. You are a joy to me."

In a word, Pop's touch affirmed me. At an early age, I experienced the power of a father's touch. Pop's hand became the signature over my soul. I never hungered for his love and affection. I guess I always knew I had it. Although as I was growing up, he could never bring himself to say "I love you," I knew the reality of his love.

> *There are many ways that we can reach out and touch our children.*

A few Christian friends have said to me through the years, "Crawford, are you sure that you didn't have an empty spot in your heart and life because while you were growing up your dad never said, 'I love you'?" In all honesty, I never felt such emptiness, because Pop said it in so many different ways that I never doubted his love. He never *verbally* said it, but we all knew how Pop felt about us.

THE BOND BETWEEN FATHER AND CHILD

There is an almost indestructible bond when a father touches his child. It extends the blessing and gives the approval that so many people spend their lives searching for. It is the connector between the generations. It says that the child is somebody and is going somewhere. It gives him his emotional address. In that sense, whenever that touch is extended the child is never far from home.

I also believe that the legitimate touch of a dad affirms

his boy's sexuality and manhood or his daughter's sexuality and womanhood. Pop gave my sisters the same collarbone rubs he gave me. And when they rubbed the bald spot on top of Pop's head, he acted as if he didn't like it, but he loved it and he'd give in to them.

Young men who grow up legitimately hungering and thirsting for proper male affection, especially that which should come from a father, sometimes seek it in other ways. They can be prime targets for those in the homosexual community who themselves never experienced the legitimate touch and tenderness from a father. Perversion is too often the tragic result. Young women who get involved in illegitimate sexual relationships often express a deep desire just to be loved and to be held. Growing up does not cancel the need for a loving touch. I hug, touch, and kiss all our children, and I tell them "I love you."

Not long ago our twenty-four-year-old son, Bryan, and I were having dinner at the Atlanta airport. He had to fly back to Los Angeles where he's finishing his master's degree. As we were saying our good-byes, right there in the middle of the atrium with hundreds of people walking past, I hugged him, prayed with him, told him that I loved him, and kissed him on his cheek. He kind of pulled away, smiled, and said, "Dad, you've got to remember where you are." But his smile told me, "It's really OK. I still love and look forward to your touch."

TOUCHES OF LOVE

It goes beyond just the physical touch. I think there are many ways that we can reach out and touch our children. Our oldest kids, Bryan and Heather, are in college, and I write them once a week just to let them know how much I love them. I want them to hear how much they are on my heart and mind. I want them to always know that they occupy the center stage in my life. I want my touch to let them know that they have access to my heart, regardless of the things that I want them to do, what I want them to be, the kinds of grades that I want them to have, or what place I want them to occupy in the world.

A touch says you don't have to do anything but just be who you are, and that's enough for me to love you, affirm you, and accept you. Karen and I try never to end a phone conversation with our children (or with each other) without saying the magic words "I love you." We want our kids to know that we are always here for them. We touch them with our words, we touch them with our hands, and we try to touch them by allowing them access to our lives.

LEARNING TO SAY "I LOVE YOU"

But do you know what? Even though he was indeed a product of his time in some ways, something amazing happened in my father's life. As I said earlier, Pop was a tender touch. Underneath all of his bravado and macho image, there was a really tender heart. And at the end of his life, Pop learned to express his love in words.

When Pop was seventy-five, his health really began to plummet, and he had to have emergency heart surgery. Because of his failing health, this was quite an ordeal. We didn't know if he was going to make it, but there weren't too many alternatives to surgery. There were a number of challenging personal affairs that I had to take care of for Mom and him during this time; she obviously was preoccupied with Pop's situation. God in his graciousness preserved Pop's life and the operation was a success. I came back from Roanoke to Atlanta and became immersed in my schedule and activities.

After he recovered, Pop called me at my office. He never called *anybody*, so when my assistant told me that my father was on the line, several thoughts raced across my mind. First,

I thought, *Maybe it's Mom calling on behalf of Pop.* Then I remember thinking the worst. I thought for sure that if it was indeed Pop, the only reason he would be dialing a telephone was to tell me that my mother had died. I scooped up the phone. Sure enough, it was Pop on the other end of the line.

I asked him, "Is everything OK?"

"Everything's fine."

"Are you sure?"

"Yes."

"Is Mom OK?"

"Yes." And then he paused.

I said, "Pop, what's going on?"

It seemed like an eternity, and then all of a sudden I heard his voice break with emotion as he said the words that had taken him almost forty years to say: "Son, I love you."

It was worth the wait, but so precious to me that it only drove my conviction deeper to tell my own children "I love you" as often as I can. Try it. The legacy starts now, and can only grow well in terms of courage, wisdom, and accountability if it is bathed in love.

As he got on in years, I would sometimes hear Pop whisper in his children's, grandchildren's, and great-grandchildren's ears, "I love you." I did not see my dad cry much at all when we were growing up, but as we would visit him as a family with our kids, he hated to see us go. In fact, I would glance at him when it came time to say good-bye, and there would often be a tear rolling down his cheek.

It's very hard telling this even now. There would be a tear rolling down Pop's cheek, and he would pull his grandchildren close to him. They would all gather around "Pop-Pop" and kiss him on his head, and I would hear him say really quietly, "I love you." Inevitably Karen and I had a hard time when we would leave. We often drove back home with our eyes full of tears too, to hear the old warrior say those words to his legacy.

Questions and Application

1. How often do you verbally tell your children "I love you"? How often do you say those words to your spouse?
2. How often do you touch your children to affirm them? Ask them what their favorite touches from you are.
3. What were your favorite touches to receive growing up? Take some time to tell your family about them.

APPENDIX A

EXTENDING
THE BLESSING

I've just told you how important encouragement and affirmation is in the lives of your children. With their permission, allow me to share these letters I wrote to Bryan and Heather to release them into a new stage of adulthood. Bryan's letter celebrates his college graduation; Heather's, her high school graduation.

May 6, 1995

Dear Bryan,

Words cannot express the joy and pride that I feel as we celebrate this milestone in your life. I want to thank you for not giving up, for taking the "long-view," and not allowing adversity and opposition to short-cut God's process and purposes for your life. On your way to accomplishing something you have become something!

You have proved yourself to be a *man* of God. I do not mean this in a casual way. I have watched how you have handled both success and failure. You have been sensitive to God and His Word and you have grown in your ability to do the hard, difficult thing. No, I have not always agreed with your perspectives and conclusions. Yet my confidence in your desire to walk with God and to do His will has caused me to back off and respect your right and responsibility as a man to follow your conscience. I have also been impressed with how you have thoughtfully and prayerfully weighed the advice and counsel of those of us who love you and are close to you. Son, please do not lose this wonderful characteristic to humbly listen and prayerfully process the input of others. This, indeed, is the window to wisdom. Praise God, you are well on your way.

Your graduation signals a very important transition in your life. You have been commissioned into full-blown manhood. Mom and I are so very pleased because we are confident that you are ready for it. You have our every blessing and full support. We make a commitment to you that we will not interfere with you or seek to orchestrate your life in any way. We will always be available to you at any time of day or night to listen, pray, and to give advice when *you* ask. We release you to enjoy both the benefits and the consequences of your choices. As you have grown, Mom and I have gradually reduced our role as spiritual mediators between you and God. Now we stand at your side and not in front of you. You fully own the responsibility before God to walk in holiness and purity, to determine success or failure, and to develop a balanced, effective life. We will help you but you are in charge. I am confident that you can handle it!

One final word. Do not shrink back from the challenges or play it safe. You only have one life and you do not want to go to your grave wishing that you had done more or that you should have taken steps of faith. Go for it! God will not let you down. He will not fail you. For almost 25 years your mother and I have lived from God's hand to our mouths. You have grown up in an environment where daily you have seen the sovereign hand of God meet our every need. You have graduated from college debt-free. God has paid your bills. He will pay your way!

Thank you for the wonderful gift from God that you are. I find myself having to watch the pride level when I talk to others about you. You have been anointed and marked by God for your generation. We are excited to think of what God is going to do through you. Make it home before dark!

All my love,
DAD
Jer. 29:11–14

June 20, 1995

Dear Heather,

I cannot tell you how proud Mom and I are of you! Your graduation from high school is not only the launching to the next level of growth and maturity as a woman, but it is also a tremendous testimony to your commitment to Christ and your diligence as a student. You finished well, demonstrating to others and, most important, to yourself, that focus and hard work are the keys to success. Indeed, there is no secret to success. Never forget that if you are faithful then you can rely on the favor of heaven. The academic abilities you have are a gift from God. Continue to faithfully use them for His honor and glory.

Sweetheart, what warms my heart and causes me the most joy is your faithfulness to the Lord. Often I receive compliments on how well you have "turned out." My response is praise to God that *you* have made right choices. Mom and I cannot take credit for your good decisions. We may have been used of God to bring you face to face with His Word, but as you well know, no one can walk with God but you. You have chosen to surrender your life to the Lordship of Christ. As a result, He has kept you and blessed you. He has caused you to prosper. Because you made a commitment to remain sexually pure, I am convinced that God has dispatched His angels to protect you.

As you prepare to go to college this fall, do not forget how God has blessed you and kept you. He has promised to never leave you or forsake you. You will have your share of challenges and temptations. But if you stay in His Word, seek His face in consistent, believing prayer, and enter into accountability relationships with other Christians, He will protect you and lead you into victory. Do not be afraid. Take courage. The God of the ages is with you (Josh. 1:1–9)!

Mom and I believe in you. We are your number one fans. We are officially releasing you to the next level of maturity. We will serve as coaches in your life but not as controllers of your life. Over the next few years our role as coaches will diminish. We love you and we are committed to you. Before God, we will always be there when you need us and we will do whatever it takes to help you translate God's dream for your life into reality.

Girl-friend, you are the greatest. . . . Make it home before dark!

All my love,
DAD
Isa. 40

P.S. Happy Birthday!

APPENDIX B

THE SOURCE OF THE BLESSING

HAVE YOU HEARD OF THE FOUR SPIRITUAL LAWS?

Just as there are physical laws that govern the physical universe, so are there spiritual laws that govern your relationship with God.

LAW 1 *God loves you and offers a wonderful plan for your life.*

God's Love

"God so loved the world that He gave His one and only Son, that whoever believes in Him shall not perish but have eternal life" (John 3:16, NIV).

God's Plan

[Christ speaking] "I came that they might have life, and might have it abundantly" [that it might be full and meaningful] (John 10:10).

Why is it that most people are not experiencing the abundant life?

Because . . .

LAW 2 *Man is sinful and separated from God. Therefore, he cannot know and experience God's love and plan for his life.*

Man Is Sinful

"All have sinned and fall short of the glory of God" (Romans 3:23):

Man was created to have fellowship with God; but, because of his own stubborn self-will, he chose to go his own independent way and fellowship with God was broken. This self-will, characterized by an attitude of active rebellion or passive indifference, is an evidence of what the Bible calls sin.

Man Is Separated

"The wages of sin is death" [spiritual separation from God] (Romans 6:23).

HOLY GOD

SINFUL MAN

This diagram illustrates that God is holy and man is sinful. A great gulf separates the two. The arrows illustrate that man is continually trying to reach God and the abundant life through his own efforts, such as a good life, philosophy, or religion—but he inevitably fails.

The third law explains the only way to bridge this gulf . . .

LAW 3 *Jesus Christ is God's only provision for man's sin. Through Him you can know and experience God's love and plan for your life.*

He Died In Our Place
"God demonstrates His own love toward us, in that while we were yet sinners, Christ died for us" (Romans 5:8).

He Rose from the Dead
"Christ died for our sins . . . He was buried . . . He was raised on the third day, according to the Scriptures . . . He appeared to Peter, then to the twelve. After that He appeared to more than five hundred . . ." (1 Corinthians 15:3–6).

He Is the Only Way to God
"Jesus said to him, 'I am the way, and the truth, and the life; no one comes to the Father but through Me'" (John 14:6).

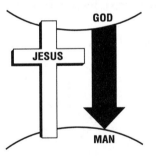

This diagram illustrates that God has bridged the gulf that separates us from Him by sending His Son, Jesus Christ, to die on the cross in our place to pay the penalty for our sins.

It is not enough just to know these three laws . . .

LAW 4 *We must individually receive Jesus Christ as Savior and Lord; then we can know and experience God's love and plan for our lives.*

We Must Receive Christ
"As many as received Him, to them He gave the right to become children of God, even to those who believe in His name" (John 1:12).

We Receive Christ Through Faith

"By grace you have been saved through faith; and that not of yourselves, it is the gift of God; not as a result of works that no one should boast" (Ephesians 2:8, 9).

When We Receive Christ, We Experience a New Birth
(Read John 3:1–8.)

We Receive Christ Through Personal Invitation

[Christ speaking] "Behold, I stand at the door and knock; if any one hears My voice and opens the door, I will come in to him" (Revelation 3:20).

Receiving Christ involves turning to God from self (repentance) and trusting Christ to come into our lives to forgive our sins and to make us what He wants us to be. Just to agree **intellectually** that Jesus Christ is the Son of God and that He died on the cross for our sins is not enough. Nor is it enough to have an **emotional** experience. We receive Jesus Christ by **faith,** as an act of the **will.**

These two circles represent two kinds of lives:

Self-Directed Life
S – Self is on the throne
†– Christ is outside the life
• – Interests are directed by self,
 often resulting in discord and frustration

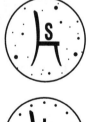

Christ-Directed Life
†– Christ is in the life and on the throne
S – Self is yielding to Christ
• –Interests are directed by Christ,
 resulting in harmony with God's plan

Which circle best represents your life?
Which circle would you like to have represent your life?
The following explains how you can receive Christ:

You Can Receive Christ Right Now by Faith Through Prayer (Prayer is talking to God)

God knows your heart and is not so concerned with your words as He is with the attitude of your heart. The following is a suggested prayer:

Lord Jesus, I need You. Thank You for dying on the cross for my sins. I open the door of my life and receive You as my Savior and Lord. Thank You for forgiving my sins and giving me eternal life. Take control of the throne of my life. Make me the kind of person You want me to be.

Does this prayer express the desire of your heart?

If it does, I invite you to pray this prayer right now, and Christ will come into your life, as He promised.

How to Know That Christ Is in Your Life

Did you receive Christ into your life? According to His promise in Revelation 3:20, where is Christ right now in relation to you? Christ said that He would come into your life. Would He mislead you? On what authority do you know that God has answered your prayer? (The trustworthiness of God Himself and His Word.)

The Bible Promises Eternal Life to All Who Receive Christ

"The witness is this, that God has given us eternal life, and this life is in His Son. He who has the Son has the life; he who does not have the Son of God does not have the life. These things I have written to you who believe in the name of the Son of God, in order that you may know that you have eternal life" (1 John 5:11–13).

Thank God often that Christ is in your life and that He will never leave you (Hebrews 13:5). You can know on the basis of His promise that Christ lives in you and that you

have eternal life from the very moment you invite Him in. He will not deceive you.

An important reminder . . .

Do Not Depend on Feelings

The promise of God's Word, the Bible—not our feelings—is our authority. The Christian lives by faith (trust) in the trust-worthiness of God Himself and His Word. This train diagram illustrates the relationship among fact (God and His Word), faith (our trust in God and His Word), and feeling (the result of our faith and obedience). (Read John 14:21.)

The train will run with or without the caboose. How-ever, it would be useless to attempt to pull the train by the caboose. In the same way, as Christians we do not depend on feelings or emotions, but we place our faith (trust) in the trustworthiness of God and the promises of His Word.

Now That You Have Received Christ

The moment you received Christ by faith, as an act of the will, many things happened, including the following:

■ Christ came into your life (Revelation 3:20; Colossians 1:27).

■ Your sins were forgiven (Colossians 1:14).

■ You became a child of God (John 1:12).

■ You received eternal life (John 5:24).

■ You began the great adventure for which God created you (John 10:10; 2 Corinthians 5:17; 1 Thessalonians 5:18).

Can you think of anything more wonderful that could happen to you than receiving Christ? Would you like to thank God in prayer right now for what He has done for you? By thanking God, you demonstrate your faith.

To enjoy your new life to the fullest . . .

Suggestions for Christian Growth
Spiritual growth results from trusting Jesus Christ. "The righteous man shall live by faith" (Galatians 3:11). A life of faith will enable you to trust God increasingly with every detail of your life, and to practice the following:

Go to God in prayer daily (John 15:7).
Read God's Word daily (Acts 17:11); begin with the Gospel of John.
Obey God moment by moment (John 14:21).
Witness for Christ by your life and words (Matthew 4:19; John 15:8).
Trust God for every detail of your life (1 Peter 5:7).
Holy Spirit—allow Him to control and empower your daily life and witness (Galatians 5:16, 17; Acts 1:8).

Fellowship in a Good Church
God's Word instructs us not to forsake "the assembling of ourselves together" (Hebrews 10:25). Several logs burn brightly together, but put one aside on the cold hearth and the fire goes out. So it is with your relationship with other Christians.

If you do not belong to a church, do not wait to be invited. Take the initiative; call the pastor of a nearby church where Christ is honored and His Word is preached. Start this week, and make plans to attend regularly.

Special Materials Are Available for Christian Growth
If you have come to know Christ personally through this presentation of the gospel, helpful materials for Christian growth are available to you. For more information, write Campus Crusade for Christ, 100 Sunport Lane 2100, Orlando, FL 32809.

SINCE 1894, Moody Publishers has been dedicated to equip and motivate people to advance the cause of Christ by publishing evangelical Christian literature and other media for all ages, around the world. Because we are a ministry of the Moody Bible Institute of Chicago, a portion of the proceeds from the sale of this book go to train the next generation of Christian leaders.

If we may serve you in any way in your spiritual journey toward understanding Christ and the Christian life, please contact us at www.moodypublishers.com.

*"All Scripture is God-breathed and is useful
for teaching, rebuking, correcting and training in
righteousness, so that the man of God may be
thoroughly equipped for every good work."*
—2 TIMOTHY 3:16, 17

MOODY
PUBLISHERS

THE NAME YOU CAN TRUST®

More Insights from Moody Publishers and Crawford Loritts

ISBN: 0-8024-5437-2

Crawford Loritts wants you to know that what is often passed off as repentance has nothing to do with what the Scriptures say repentance is. He also wants you to know that only a true understanding of its reality can bring us into an authentic relationship with God.

What a needed book! Make It Home Before Dark *is one of those rare books that I intend to give to my friends. Crawford's book will change your perspective about repentance and as a result, you'll experience the love of God in a fresh way.*
> Dennis Rainey
> Executive Director, Family Life

ISBN: 0-8024-5526-3

As I read Lessons from the Life Coach, *I found myself taking notes. This book motivates me to run the race to win! But Crawford is more than a great life coach — he's one of my close friends.*
> Dennis Rainey
> Executive Director, Family Life

These are transforming chapters filled with promise, hope, truth, and conviction. Read on and fly above the eagles!
> Bill McCartney
> Founder/President, Promise Keepers

MOODY
PUBLISHERS
THE NAME YOU CAN TRUST.

1-800-678-6928 www.MoodyPublishers.org